Better Words
A First Thesaurus

by

C. Windridge

©**1985 Schofield and Sims Ltd**

0 7217 0501 4
Net Edition 0 7217 0502 2

First Printed **1985**
Reprinted 1985, 1986, 1988, 1989, 1990, 1991, 1992, 1993

SCHOFIELD & SIMS LTD, HUDDERSFIELD

Notes for the teacher

Better Words is a first thesaurus which is aimed at the child with a mental age of nine years; and, therefore, it caters for the thesaurus needs of children of all abilities within the chronological 7 to 11 age-range. The notes 'Using this book' (page 4) explain how the thesaurus should be used. Its main purpose is to persuade children to avoid over-using words such as **get, nice, big** and **good**, which form a large part of their vocabulary, and to use better words instead; that is to say, words which would be more suitable as a means of correct and elegant expression. In this way children will enlarge and enrich their vocabulary and develop their ability to speak and write more accurately and more stylishly, and so more effectively. As a secondary purpose it provides children with some rudimentary knowledge of grammar – the parts of speech – and they should soon become very adept at identifying a word as a particular part of speech. Another purpose, and one that is by no means unimportant, is to introduce children to the correct use of a thesaurus and to encourage them to acquire skill and familiarity in its use, so that, at a later stage, they will be able to use Choose your Words, a more elaborate thesaurus designed for the 9 to 13 age-range and, ultimately, perhaps, Roget's Thesaurus, with complete confidence and practised ease.

Taken together, the basic lists of synonyms and antonyms provide a wide choice from a total of about 8000 words. If a word has an alternative spelling, as, for example, **grey/gray**, or **realize/realise,** only the preferable form is given so that the child will come to possess good spelling habits at an early age.

However, this general rule does not apply in those few cases where the alternative spellings are equally acceptable, as with **inquire** and **enquire**. Here, both forms are given.

How to Better Your Words   07217 0503 0

This companion set of exercises to Better Words has been carefully designed to help pupils to improve their "word power" and become skilful in using a thesaurus. It is strongly recommended that the children perform all the exercises in *How to Better Your Words* if they are to become proficient in using a thesaurus.

Contents

Using this book

Please read these notes very carefully.

What is a thesaurus?

A thesaurus is a special word book that helps you to use words which are better, that is, more stylish or more exact than the words you usually use in your own speech and writing.

Sames and similars

Some words have the same meaning, as, for example, wonderful and marvellous. These words are called *synonyms*. Some other words are similar, but not exactly the same, in meaning, as, for example, absent and away.

This book contains a list of words that are the same or similar in meaning. This list is arranged in three columns. The first column contains an alphabetical list of everyday words, most of which you already know. These are the words to which you refer. The second column contains the abbreviations that are used to show the parts of speech. The third column contains the words that are the same or similar in meaning to those words in the first column. From these words you can choose the word that is best for your purpose. Some of the words in the first column have more than one meaning. In these cases, the words that follow are shown in separate groups, each of which is numbered, as, for example:

air	*n*	1 atmosphere
		2 appearance, manner, style
		3 tune
	v	dry, warm, ventilate
		She hung the damp clothes on the line to **air**.

Abbreviations

These abbreviations are used to show the parts of speech:

n	noun	*pron*	pronoun	*adj*	adjective	*v*	verb
adv	adverb	*conj*	conjunction	*prep*	preposition	*int*	interjection

The parts of speech

Some words are more than one part of speech. For example, *alight* is both a verb, meaning *dismount*, and an adjective meaning *burning*.

You should now read the next section (page 5) which will tell you about the parts of speech.

Opposites

Words that are opposite in meaning, such as night and day, good and bad, are called *antonyms*. At the end of this book, there is a list of words which are opposite in meaning (pages 118 to 126).

Also, at the end of this book, there are some useful facts about making opposites of words.

The parts of speech

The work that a word does in a sentence is called a part of speech. There are eight parts of speech. They are listed below – with some common examples and a few sample sentences.

noun n A noun is a name. It may be an object, a place, an animal, a person or a quality. **Examples** banana London monkey Richard kindness *Richard* is a *man* of great *kindness*.	**adverb** adv An adverb tells us more about a verb or an adjective. **Examples** very quickly angrily soon calmly *Quickly* and *angrily,* the *very* hungry tiger *soon* ran towards us.
pronoun pron A pronoun can take the place of a noun. **Examples** they him she it one *Mary* gave the *book* to *Peter.* *She* gave *it* to *him.* People do not care. *One* does not care.	**conjunction** conj A conjunction joins words, or two or more simple sentences to make a single sentence. **Examples** and but because either or Peter *and* Charles were very unhappy *because* they had not won the race.
adjective adj An adjective tells us more about a noun or a pronoun. **Examples** beautiful selfish big rich heavy The piano was *big* and *heavy.* She was *rich* and *beautiful* but *selfish.*	**preposition** prep A preposition joins a noun to the rest of the sentence. **Examples** in from to at towards John walked *from* Birmingham *to* Coventry. Charles, *in* his hurry, ran quickly *towards* us.
verb v A verb tells us about what is being done – it is a ''doing word''. **Examples** smile is sleep lives shines The sky *is* blue and the sun *shines* brightly. Mary *lives* in London.	**interjection** int An interjection shows surprise. It could be any word. **Examples** oh ah ouch what goodness ''*oh, goodness,* what next?'' he said angrily. ''*What!* there is no food left?'' she shouted.

Aa

aback   *adv*   backwards, rearwards, behind
taken aback surprised, shocked

abandon   *v*   give up, leave, depart from, desert, forsake, vacate, evacuate

abandoned   *adj*   given up, derelict, deserted, forsaken, vacated, vacant, empty, rejected

abide   *v*   1 dwell, stay, live, reside, lodge, rest, remain, wait
2 suffer, put up with, bear, endure, stand, accept

ability   *n*   skill, talent, cleverness, power

ablaze   *adj*   on fire, in flame, burning, glittering

able   *adj*   skilful, talented, clever, smart

aboard   *prep*   on, on to, on board, in, into, inside
He jumped **aboard** the train.

abode   *n*   dwelling, home, residence

abolish   *v*   do away with, end, finish, destroy, ban, bar, eliminate, remove

abound   *v*   be rich, be plentiful, teem, overflow

about   *prep*   of, to do with, concerning
    adv   1 round, around, all round
2 almost, nearly

abreast   *adv*   1 side by side
They walked two or three **abreast**.
2 up-to-date

abroad   *adv*   far away, in a foreign land, in another country
Mary lives **abroad**.

abrupt   *adj*   sudden, unexpected, hurried, quick, hasty, sharp, short, blunt

absent   *adj*   away, not present, lacking
    v   stay away

absent-minded   *adj*   inattentive, forgetful, dreamy, not alert, careless, unwary

absurd   *adj*   silly, ridiculous, foolish, senseless, crazy, stupid, odd, strange, unreasonable

abundant	*adj*	plentiful, rich, overflowing, teeming, generous
abuse	*v*	use wrongly, harm, damage, injure, ill-treat, treat badly, insult
	n	wrongful use, damage, injury Litter is an **abuse** of the countryside.
accept	*v*	take, receive, allow, agree to, admit, approve of, believe
access	*n*	way in, entrance, doorway, opening, approach
accident	*n*	1 mishap, misfortune, injury 2 unexpected event, chance
accompany	*v*	go with, escort, guide, support
accomplish	*v*	do, manage, perform, achieve, succeed in doing
account	*n*	1 report, story, description 2 invoice, bill 3 reason, cause, explanation
	v	explain, give reason, find cause
accumulate	*v*	gather, collect, assemble, save, hoard, store
accurate	*adj*	exact, correct, true, truthful, honest, reliable, precise
accuse	*v*	blame, charge
ache	*n*	1 lasting pain 2 longing, great desire, yearning
achieve	*v*	gain, win, get, obtain, reach, carry out, accomplish, attain
acid	*adj*	sour, tart, harsh, severe, sharp, vinegary, bitter
acquire	*v*	gain, obtain, get, receive, win, take, achieve
act	*n*	1 deed, feat, action, law, decree 2 part (of a stage play), performance
	v	1 do, behave, perform, work 2 pretend, sham
action	*n*	act, deed, performance, work, motion, movement, activity, battle

Aa

active	*adj*	quick, quick-moving, rapid, fast, swift, lively, brisk, nimble, agile, busy, hard-working, energetic, industrious
actual	*adj*	real, true, genuine, existing, certain
acute	*adj*	1 sharp, pointed 2 high, shrill 3 keen, sensitive, sharp, quick 4 severe, serious
adequate	*adj*	enough, sufficient, suitable, proper, satisfactory
adjust	*v*	change, alter, adapt, arrange
admire	*v*	respect, approve of, like, praise, appreciate
admission	*n*	1 admittance, entrance, access 2 confession
admit	*v*	1 accept, allow, acknowledge 2 confess, declare 3 allow to enter
ado	*n*	fuss, bustle, difficulty
adopt	*v*	choose, take, take over, accept, pick, select
adore	*v*	love, cherish, admire, worship
adrift	*adv*	1 drifting, out of control 2 unsettled, unfastened
adult	*n* *adj*	grown-up person grown-up, mature
advance	*v*	progress, go forward, approach
advantage	*n*	help, benefit
advice	*n*	guidance, opinion, counsel
advise	*v*	guide, recommend, inform, notify, tell
afar	*adv*	at/from a distance, in a distant land
affair	*n*	matter, business, event
affection	*n*	love, liking, fondness, tenderness, regard
afire	*adj*	in flame, flaming, on fire, burning

aflame	*adj*	in flame, flaming, on fire, afire, burning
afloat	*adv*	floating, at sea, on board ship
afoot	*adv*	1 on the move, astir 2 happening He wondered what was **afoot**.
afraid	*adj*	frightened, scared, alarmed, in fear, fearful, timid, uneasy
afterwards, afterward	*adv*	later on
age	*n* *v*	long time, long period grow older, become old
agile	*adj*	quick, quick-moving, lively, nimble, brisk, active, rapid, fast
agog	*adj*	eager, excited, expectant, impatient We were **agog** to hear the story.
agony	*n*	great pain, anguish, torment, suffering
agree	*v*	approve, allow, accept, consent, grant
agreeable	*adj*	pleasant, pleasing, tasteful, acceptable, satisfactory, willing
agreement	*n*	promise, bargain, contract
ahead	*adv*	in advance, in front, before, forward
aid	*n* *v*	help, assistance, grant help, assist, support
ailment	*n*	illness, sickness, affliction
aim	*n* *v*	purpose, intention, object, target, goal, end, ambition His **aim** was to win. 1 intend 2 direct, take aim at, level, point
air	*n* *v*	1 atmosphere 2 appearance, manner, style 3 tune dry, warm, ventilate She **aired** the damp clothes on the line.
akin	*adj*	similar, related

Aa

alarm   *n*   1 warning, alert
        2 fear, fright, panic, excitement
    v   1 warn, alert, make aware
        2 frighten, disturb, startle, excite

alert   *n*   warning, alarm
    adj   attentive, wide-awake, wary, watchful, lively, active
    v   warn, alarm

alight   *adj*   lighted, on fire, burning, in flame, aflame
    v   get down, dismount, descend, settle

alike   *adj*   like, similar, resembling
    adv   similarly, in the same way

all   *adj*   the whole number of
    adv   wholly, completely
    n   everyone, everything

allow   *v*   1 let, permit, consent to, agree to, accept, stand, suffer, bear, put up with, tolerate, give, award, bestow
        2 admit, own, agree, confess, declare, acknowledge, grant

almost   *adv*   nearly, all but

aloft   *adv*   above, overhead, upward, upwards

alone   *adj*   lone, lonely, solitary, by itself
    adv   only

also   *adv*   too, besides, as well, in addition, furthermore, what is more

alter   *v*   change, vary, adjust, rearrange, amend

although   *conj*   though, if, even if

altogether   *adv*   entirely, on the whole, wholly, totally, completely, fully

amaze   *v*   surprise, astonish, astound, dumbfound

ambition   *n*   desire, hope, aim, target, goal, objective

amiable   *adj*   lovable, friendly, likeable, agreeable, good-natured, good-tempered, pleasant

amid, amidst   *prep*   in the middle of, among, amongst

among, amongst	*prep*	amid, amidst, mixed with
amount	*n* *v*	quantity, number, total come to, add up to
ample	*adj*	enough, sufficient, generous, abundant, plentiful, extensive
amuse	*v*	entertain, cause laughter, act comically, please
anger	*n*	rage, wrath, temper, fury
angle	*n*	corner, sharp bend
angry	*adj*	annoyed, vexed, furious, cross, indignant, offended, enraged, irritated
animal	*n*	beast, brute, creature
announce	*v*	tell, declare, report, reveal, advertise, proclaim, broadcast
annoy	*v*	anger, exasperate, irritate, bother, pester, tease, vex
annual	*adj*	yearly
anonymous	*adj*	nameless, unknown
another	*adj*	one more, different, an extra He brought **another** friend.
answer	*n*	1 solution, result 2 reply, retort
antic	*n*	game, prank, trick
anxiety	*n*	worry, concern, uneasiness, alarm, anguish, fear
apart	*adv*	aside, separately **set apart** put on one side, reserve
ape	*v* *n*	mimic, copy, imitate tailless monkey
apparel	*n*	dress, clothing, garments, attire, costume, robes
appeal	*v*	request, beg, ask, pray, plead, entreat, implore, beseech

Aa

appear	*v*	1 emerge, become visible, come into sight 2 look, seem, show
applaud	*v*	praise, cheer, shout for, clap
approve	*v*	accept, like, allow, permit, agree to, confirm, sanction
apt	*adj*	suitable, appropriate
argue	*v*	differ, dispute, discuss, debate, reason
arms	*n*	1 upper limbs (of humans), branches, cross-pieces 2 weapons
arouse	*v*	awaken, waken, rouse, excite, stir into action
arrange	*v*	1 order, group, sort, select, adapt 2 plan, prepare, organize
arrest	*v*	1 stop, halt, check, delay 2 catch, hold, seize, capture, take prisoner
arrive	*v*	come, reach
artful	*adj*	cunning, crafty, sly, wily, deceitful
article	*n*	object, item, thing
ascend	*v*	rise, go up, come up, climb, mount
ashen	*adj*	pale, wan
ask	*v*	1 request, invite, call for, demand, require 2 inquire (enquire), question, call for an answer **ask after** inquire about (a person)
assemble	*v*	1 fit together, build, construct 2 gather together, collect, meet, throng, rally
assist	*v*	help, aid, support
assortment	*n*	mixture, collection, variety, selection
assume	*v*	suppose, pretend, act, take for granted

astonish	*v*	astound, surprise, amaze, shock, dumbfound, startle
astound	*v*	astonish, surprise, amaze, shock, dumbfound, alarm
astray	*adv*	wandering, missing **gone astray** lost, mislaid
attach	*v*	fasten, fix, connect, join
attack	*v*	assault, fall upon, do battle with, storm, charge
	n	bout, spell, fit
attempt	*v*	try, endeavour, strive
	n	effort, endeavour, try
attire	*n*	dress, clothing, apparel, garments, costume
attract	*v*	draw to, draw forwards, bring near, please, excite, entice, charm
avail	*v*	help, benefit
	n	value, profit, use His efforts were of no **avail**.
available	*adj*	near, handy, within reach
average	*adj*	normal, usual, standard, common, ordinary, everyday
avoid	*v*	escape, dodge, keep away from, evade
avow	*v*	admit, acknowledge, confess
await	*v*	wait for, expect
awake	*v*	awaken, wake, wake up, arouse, rouse, bestir
aware	*adj*	knowing, conscious, mindful, watchful, observant
away	*adv*	1 at a distance, in another place, not present 2 without delay
awe	*n*	wonder, respect, fear, reverence
awful	*adj*	terrible, dreadful, frightening
awkward	*adj*	clumsy, unskilful, ungainly, difficult, not easy, risky, embarrassing, inconvenient
aye	*adv*	1 yes 2 always, for ever

Bb

babble	v	prattle, gabble, chatter, murmur, speak babyishly
baby	n	infant, young child
babyish	adj	infantile, childish, silly
back	n	rear, reverse side
	v	1 support, assist, help 2 go back, move backwards, reverse 3 bet, gamble
backbone	n	1 spine 2 courage, grit
backward	adj	1 slow, dull, shy, reluctant 2 rearward, reversed, in reverse
	adv	backwards, rearward, behind, aback
bad	adj	1 naughty, mischievous, wicked, badly-behaved, unruly, disobedient, rude, wrong, dreadful, unseemly, evil, vile, sinful, shocking, destructive 2 poor, faulty, unsatisfactory, disgusting, unpleasant, distasteful, harmful, horrible, poisonous, tainted, unwholesome, decayed, rotten 3 ill, sick, ailing, unwell, poorly
badge	n	mark, sign, emblem, crest
baffle	v	mystify, bewilder, perplex, puzzle, confuse, foil
baggage	n	bags, cases, luggage, belongings
bait	v	worry, bother, trouble, annoy, tease, torment
	n	lure (trap or hook), enticement
balance	v	make equal, match, poise, weigh
	n	1 poise, steadiness, stability 2 scales, weighing-machine
ball	n	1 sphere, globe, orb 2 dance, social gathering
ban	v	forbid, bar, not permit, quash, disqualify, make an end to, prohibit
band	n	1 group, gang, company, troop, pack, flock, herd 2 strip, stripe, border, bar, ribbon

bandit	*n*	brigand, robber, outlaw, criminal, crook, gangster, highwayman
bang	*n*	1 loud noise, loud sound, burst, explosion, report, crash 2 bump, thump, blow, knock, thud, slam
	v	strike, beat, shut noisily
banish	*v*	exile, send away, remove from, cast out, outlaw, drive away
bar	*v*	forbid, ban, not allow, disqualify, prohibit, fasten, obstruct
	n	1 beam, rod, pole, counter 2 strip, stripe, line, band
bard	*n*	poet, minstrel
bare	*adj*	naked, bald, uncovered, unclothed, nude, empty, scanty, meagre, mere
barely	*adv*	merely, scarcely, only just, hardly, not quite
barren	*adj*	fruitless, empty, bare, infertile
barrier	*n*	barricade, gate, fence, hedge, wall, obstruction, blockage, hindrance
barter	*v*	exchange, swap, trade
base	*n*	bottom, foot, foundation, support, starting-point
	adj	low, vulgar, mean, despised, selfish, vile, worthless
bashful	*adj*	shy, easily embarrassed, shamefaced, sheepish
battle	*n*	conflict, fight, struggle, combat, action
	v	fight, struggle
beam	*n*	1 bar, girder, cross-piece, balance, square timber, rod 2 ray, signal, smile
bear	*v*	1 carry, support, hold, transport, produce 2 suffer, put up with, abide, stand, endure, tolerate
beast	*n*	animal, brute, creature

Bb

beat	*v*	1 strike, bang, thrash, hit, batter 2 defeat, vanquish, conquer, outwit 3 throb, pulsate
	n	stroke, bang, pulse
beauteous	*adj*	beautiful, lovely, fair, pretty, handsome, good-looking, fine
beautiful	*adj*	fair, lovely, pretty, handsome, attractive, charming, good-looking, delightful, splendid, comely, elegant, graceful, fine, pleasing
become	*v*	1 change to, change into, begin to be 2 suit, befit, grace Bad manners do not **become** a princess.
becoming	*adj*	suitable, fitting, befitting, attractive
before	*adv*	in front, in advance, ahead, earlier, beforehand, already
beg	*v*	ask for, request, implore, plead, pray, appeal to, entreat, beseech
beggarly	*adj*	1 very small, little, slight, trifling, mean, meagre, miserly 2 poor, shabby
begin	*v*	commence, start, introduce
behind	*adv*	behindhand, in the rear, backward, backwards, to the back, after, afterwards, late
belief	*n*	knowledge, faith, trust, thought, confidence, opinion
belly	*n*	abdomen, bowels
belly-ache	*n*	stomach-ache, colic, abdominal pains
belongings	*n*	personal property, baggage, luggage, possessions
beloved	*adj* *n*	much loved, dearest, cherished loved one, darling, dearest one
below	*adv*	under, underneath, beneath, downstairs, at a lower level, downstream
	prep	lower or lesser than (in size, position or rank), to or at a greater depth than

bend	*v*	1 turn, curve, twist 2 bow, stoop
	n	curve, angle, turning
beneath	*adv*	under, underneath, below
benefit	*n*	advantage, gain, profit, help, aid
	v	help, aid, assist, profit
beside	*prep*	close to, nearby, on a level with, alongside, adjacent to, next to
besides	*adv*	also, in addition, furthermore, moreover
best	*adj*	finest, most suitable, appropriate
betroth	*v*	promise to wed
better	*adj*	improved, preferable, more desirable
	v	improve, amend, correct
bewilder	*v*	mystify, baffle, puzzle, perplex, confuse, muddle
beyond	*prep*	out of reach of, past, outside
	adv	at a distance, past, outside
bicker	*v*	quarrel, differ, argue, wrangle, dispute, squabble
bid	*v*	1 offer, invite, ask 2 greet, salute, acknowledge I **bid** you goodnight. 3 order, command, summon
big	*adj*	large, great, grand, huge, giant, gigantic, vast, immense, enormous, tremendous, enlarged, swollen, important, bulky, massive, mighty
bill	*n*	1 notice, poster, leaflet, placard 2 beak, muzzle 3 invoice, account
bind	*v*	join, fasten, hold together, tie, secure
bit	*n*	small piece, part, portion, fraction, fragment, morsel, chip, splinter
bite	*v*	nip, sting, cut, grip (with teeth)
bitter	*adj*	not sweet, biting, harsh, severe, unpleasant, disappointed
blame	*v*	accuse, charge, censure, reproach

Bb

blank   *adj*   empty, vacant, not printed on, not written on

blaze   *n*   bright flame, bright fire
    v   burn brightly

bleak   *adj*   dreary, drab, dull, bare, exposed, windswept, chilly, cheerless, unsheltered, desolate

blend   *v*   mix, mingle, become one, merge, match, unite, combine
    n   mixture

blessed   *adj*   holy, sacred, revered, lucky, fortunate, well-favoured, consecrated

blind   *adj*   1 without sight, sightless, unseeing
    2 not knowing, unaware, without understanding
    v   make sightless, dazzle, deceive, mislead

block   *v*   stop, obstruct, wedge, oppose, hinder, restrict, blockade

bloodthirsty   *adj*   eager for bloodshed, cruel, brutal, savage, bestial, barbarous

bloom   *n*   1 blossom, flower
    2 freshness, youthfulness, innocence

blot   *n*   spot, stain, mark, blemish

blow   *n*   1 knock, hit, stroke, bang, thump, jab, cuff, punch, rap, tap
    2 shock, mishap, misfortune, bad luck, disaster, loss, bad news
    v   puff, pant, gasp, gust

bluff   *v*   deceive, make an empty threat, pretend
    adj   1 outspoken, frank, blunt
    2 genial, friendly, hearty

blunder   *v*   1 make a mistake
    2 walk clumsily, act awkwardly, stumble, trip, fall over
    n   mistake, error, foolish act, embarrassing conduct, oversight

blurred   *adj*   not clear, dim, hazy, misty, confused, indistinct, smeared, smudged

boast	*n*	brag, swagger, bravado
	v	brag, exaggerate
body	*n*	1 trunk, torso, figure, frame, form
		2 corpse, remains
		3 mass, quantity, group, company, crowd, society
bog	*n*	marsh, swamp, fen, mire, quagmire
bold	*adj*	1 forward, cheeky, unafraid, brave, daring, reckless, fearless, courageous, impudent, vigorous
		2 clear, well-marked
booty	*n*	plunder, loot, profit, prize, treasure
border	*n*	edge, margin, dividing line, brink, boundary, frontier, side
bore	*v*	drill, pierce, make a hole in
	n	1 dull person, uninteresting activity, drudge
		2 hole, internal diameter
		3 tidal wave
bottle	*n*	flask, flagon, jar, vial, vessel
bottom	*n*	base, foot, lowest part, posterior
bough	*n*	branch, arm, limb
bound	*n*	1 leap, jump, spring, gambol, skip
		2 limit, boundary, restriction, rule
bout	*n*	1 spell, turn, fit, period
		2 contest, fight, trial of strength
bowels	*n*	belly, abdomen, intestines
branch	*n*	bough, arm, limb, line, offshoot
bravado	*n*	defiance, display of bravery, pretended courage
brave	*adj*	courageous, bold, daring, fearless, plucky, valiant, heroic, gallant
bravery	*n*	courage, valour, boldness
brawny	*adj*	strong, powerful, muscular
break	*v*	crack, split, shatter, fracture, damage, spoil
		break down fall, collapse
		break into enter

Bb

brief	*adj*	short, concise, terse, curt
bright	*adj*	1 shining, gleaming, brilliant, lit up, dazzling, glowing, glossy, light, luminous, sunny, vivid 2 clever, smart, alert, intelligent, quick-witted, talented
brilliant	*adj*	1 bright, shining, gleaming, sparkling 2 very clever, intelligent, talented, gifted
bring	*v*	carry, bear, transport, fetch, lead, guide, convey
brink	*n*	edge, border, brim, verge
brisk	*adj*	quick, quick-moving, rapid, fast, swift, lively, active
brittle	*adj*	fragile, breakable, easily broken, frail, delicate, weak
broad	*adj*	wide, not narrow, open, full, clear, complete, large, comprehensive
brutal	*adj*	bestial, beastly, cruel, savage, wild, barbarous, ruthless
build	*v*	put, fit together, assemble, erect, construct, make, manufacture, develop
bully	*v*	threaten, pester, bother, persecute
bump	*n*	1 noise, sound, bang, thud, thump 2 blow, rap, hit, stroke, jolt, collision
bumptious	*adj*	conceited, vain, proud, boastful
bunch	*n*	cluster, handful, group
burden	*n*	1 load, weight 2 worry, problem, anxiety
burly	*adj*	strong, tough, sturdy
burn	*v*	set on fire, ignite, blaze, flame, consume (by fire), incinerate
burst	*v*	fly apart, split open, explode, collapse
business	*n*	1 matter, affair, concern 2 job, work, trade, employment, occupation, profession, task

busy	*adj*	active, occupied, working, employed, engaged
busybody	*n*	meddler, interfering person, mischief-maker
but	*conj* *prep*	however, whereas, despite that except, except for, apart from No one **but** Jane could do it.
butcher	*v*	kill, slaughter, slay, murder, massacre, exterminate
buy	*v*	purchase
bystander	*n*	onlooker, spectator, witness, observer

Cc

café	*n*	tea-shop, restaurant, snack-bar
calculate	*v*	work out, reckon, estimate, count, determine, assess, compute, plan, forecast
call	*v*	1 shout, cry, hail, greet, signal, announce 2 name, address as, know as 3 send for, summon, invite, call
callous	*adj*	unfeeling, hard-hearted
calm	*adj*	gentle, peaceful, quiet, still, tame, untroubled, relaxed, composed, serene, tranquil, unruffled, windless
camouflage	*v*	disguise, hide, conceal, cover, mask, obscure
cancel	*v*	cross out, remove, withdraw, delete, erase, abolish
capable	*adj*	able, skilful, efficient, clever, talented, competent
capital	*adj* *n*	1 chief, main, principal, largest, leading, most important 2 fine, excellent, splendid, superb main city, chief city
capsize	*v*	overturn, tip over, upset
captain	*n*	1 commander, leader, chief, head 2 master, skipper
capture	*v*	catch, seize, trap, grasp, hold, grab, take, get, snare, ensnare, arrest, attract
car	*n*	motor car, automobile, vehicle
care	*n*	1 attention, interest, trouble, pains 2 concern, worry, anxiety 3 caution, watchfulness, wariness, attention
career	*n* *v*	profession, calling go swiftly, run wildly
careful	*adj*	attentive, cautious, heedful, mindful, prudent, thoughtful, wary, watchful, painstaking

careless	*adj*	uncaring, thoughtless, not careful, imprudent, unmindful, negligent, unwary, reckless, unconcerned
cargo	*n*	goods, load, shipment, freight
carry	*v*	convey, transport, transfer, bear
case	*n*	1 container, box, holder, crate, chest 2 event, affair, matter, business, example, instance 3 lawsuit
cast	*v* *n*	1 throw, pitch, toss, heave, fling 2 drop, shed, let fall 3 mould, shape, form actors, performers
casual	*adj*	informal, uncaring, careless, easygoing
catch	*v*	grasp, hold, seize, get, grip, capture, take, trap, snare, ensnare, arrest, entangle
cause	*n* *v*	reason, purpose, start, beginning, origin start, begin, force, compel, originate
cautious	*adj*	careful, mindful, prudent, watchful, needful, wary, discreet
cease	*v*	stop, end, finish, conclude, discontinue
celebrate	*v*	make merry, rejoice, honour, observe, praise
centre	*n*	middle, midst, core, heart, kernel, axis
ceremony	*n*	celebration, occasion, function, rite, custom
certain	*adj*	1 sure, definite, without doubt, convinced 2 particular, actual, existing
challenge	*v*	dare, defy, question, oppose
champion	*n* *adj* *v*	1 victor, winner 2 defender, supporter, protector unbeaten, best, supreme defend, uphold
chance	*n*	1 risk, gamble, opportunity 2 luck, fortune, fate, accident

Cc

change	*v*	alter, adjust, vary, transform, exchange, substitute
chaos	*n*	disorder, confusion, panic, turmoil, tumult
char	*v*	burn, scorch, blacken
character	*n*	1 nature, quality, kind, type, sort 2 reputation 3 person
charge	*n*	1 attack, stampede, rush 2 accusation 3 price, cost, amount **in charge** responsible
charm	*v*	please, delight, attract, entice, enchant, entrance, bewitch
	n	1 good-luck token, lucky trinket, magic spell 2 attraction, quality, fascination
chart	*n*	map, plan, diagram
chat	*v*	talk, gossip, chatter
chatter	*v*	jabber, prattle, gabble, babble
cheap	*adj*	not dear, not costly, low-priced, inferior, inexpensive
cheat	*v*	deceive, trick, swindle, defraud, snare
check	*v*	1 slow down, hinder, stop, restrain, arrest, halt 2 test, examine, inspect, investigate
cheek	*n*	impertinence, impudence, sauce
chest	*n*	1 breast, bosom 2 case, box, crate, container, coffer
chief	*adj*	main, principal, head, most important, largest, leading
	n	head, director, leader, captain, ruler, chieftain
child	*n*	infant, baby, bairn
chill	*v*	cool, make cold, refrigerate
	adj	cold, chilly, unfeeling, frigid
	n	cold, coolness
chip	*n*	tiny piece, small chunk, splinter, fragment

choke	v	smother, strangle, stifle, suffocate
choose	v	pick, select, prefer, favour, elect, opt
chop	v	cut, hack, chip, slash, hew, mince
chum	n	friend, mate, pal, companion, comrade
circle	n	ring, band
	v	surround, revolve
civil	adj	courteous, polite, well-mannered, obliging
claim	v	ask for, demand, contend
clash	v	1 differ, contrast 2 disagree, quarrel, dispute
clasp	v	clamp, grip, clutch, grasp, grab, snatch, hold, embrace
	n	hook, catch, fastener
class	n	group, set, grade, kind, sort, type, category, selection, rank, quality
clean	v	wash, tidy, cleanse, launder, scour, scrub
	adj	spotless, pure, fresh
clear	adj	1 plain, distinct, bright, cloudless, transparent, obvious, apparent 2 open, unobstructed
clever	adj	smart, bright, intelligent, expert, gifted, able, talented, wise, skilful, skilled, ingenious, capable
climb	v	ascend, mount, scale
cling	v	hold, clasp, clutch, stick, adhere
cloak	n	1 coat, mantle, wrap, shawl 2 cover, pretence, disguise
close	v	1 shut, seal, cover 2 end, finish, complete, conclude
	adv	near, adjoining, adjacent
clothe	v	cover, dress, attire
clothing	n	clothes, garments, apparel, garb, dress, attire, costume

Cc

cloud	*v*	darken, obscure
clown	*n*	jester, buffoon, joker, fool, comic
club	*n*	1 stick, baton, bat, cudgel, truncheon 2 group, circle, society, association
clue	*n*	hint, guide, lead, key, inkling, fact
clumsy	*adj*	awkward, ungainly, bungling, unskilled, ungraceful, tactless
clutch	*v*	hold, grab, seize, snatch, clasp, clamp, grip, grasp, embrace, clench
coach	*n*	1 carriage 2 teacher, instructor, trainer, tutor
coarse	*adj*	1 not smooth, rough, harsh, matted 2 vulgar, common, uncouth, rude, loutish, ill-mannered
coat	*n*	jacket, garment, cover, covering, layer
coax	*v*	encourage, persuade, entice, tempt, wheedle
coil	*n* *v*	spiral wind, turn, encircle, wrap around, twist
cold	*adj*	1 chilly, cool, icy, freezing, frozen, frosty, keen, frigid, biting, wintry 2 distant, unfeeling, cold-blooded, unfriendly
collapse	*v*	break down, fall, fall down, give way, fail
collect	*v*	gather, pick, store, bring together, assemble, accumulate
collide	*v*	meet, hit
colossal	*adj*	gigantic, huge, massive, enormous, immense, tremendous, vast
colour	*n*	dye, paint, pigment, hue, tint
combat	*n*	fight, battle, struggle, contest, conflict, skirmish
combine	*v*	blend, join, unite, merge, mix

come	*v*	arrive, approach, advance
comfort	*n*	ease, luxury, contentment
	v	console, sympathize with, cheer up, soothe, hearten
comic	*adj*	comical, funny, amusing, humorous, laughable
command	*v*	control, direct, order, bid, instruct, rule, require, dominate, govern
commence	*v*	begin, start, initiate, originate
commit	*v*	1 do, perform 2 entrust, send
common	*adj*	ordinary, commonplace, plain, vulgar, normal, standard, everyday, average, well-known, inferior
companion	*n*	friend, chum, pal, mate, comrade
company	*n*	1 group, band, gang, crew, troop, party, gathering, assembly 2 firm, business 3 friends, companions, visitors, guests
compare	*v*	liken, match, balance
compel	*v*	force, make, drive, press, urge
competition	*n*	contest, struggle, rivalry
complain	*v*	grumble, protest, nag
complete	*v*	finish, end, conclude, terminate
	adj	whole, full, total, entire, unbroken
compress	*v*	squeeze, reduce
compute	*v*	reckon, calculate, count, number
conceal	*v*	hide, cover, disguise, mask, camouflage, keep secret
conceit	*n*	pride, vanity
concern	*n*	1 worry, anxiety, bother, interest, distress 2 affair, business, matter, scheme, plan

Cc

concerning	*prep*	about, of, to do with, concerned with
conclude	*v*	1 end, finish, complete, close, terminate 2 decide, gather, reason, judge
condition	*n*	1 state, nature, quality, grade 2 provision, agreement
conduct	*v*	1 lead, guide, escort, direct, control, manage 2 carry, transport
	n	behaviour, bearing, manner
conference	*n*	meeting, consultation
confess	*v*	admit, own up, declare, acknowledge
confident	*adj*	certain, sure, secure, hopeful, optimistic, positive
confuse	*v*	1 mix up, disturb, disarrange, jumble 2 mystify, puzzle, baffle, bewilder, perplex
connect	*v*	join, fasten, attach, tie, link, couple
conquer	*v*	beat, defeat, overcome, overpower, crush, vanquish, subdue, triumph
consent	*n*	permission, approval, agreement
	v	approve, permit, agree
consider	*v*	think about, reflect on, heed, contemplate, examine
considerable	*adj*	large, great, ample, abundant, generous, plentiful
considerate	*adj*	thoughtful, kind, unselfish, patient
constantly	*adv*	always, ceaselessly, without rest
construct	*v*	build, make, erect, put up, compile, put together, assemble, draw
consume	*v*	1 spend, waste, burn, squander 2 eat, devour, drink, swallow
contain	*v*	hold, enclose, include, comprise
content	*adj*	happy, pleased, glad, satisfied
	n	contents, filling, capacity, volume, amount

contest	*n*	struggle, competition, combat, fight
	v	dispute, compete
continue	*v*	carry on, proceed, keep up, add to, prolong, maintain, resume
contract	*v*	shorten, reduce, shrink, condense
	n	agreement, deal, document
contradict	*v*	deny, refute, dispute
control	*v*	guide, direct, manage, command, rule, drive, instruct, take charge of, conduct, curb, dominate, regulate
convenient	*adj*	suitable, handy, at hand, available
conversation	*n*	talk, chat, discussion
cool	*adj*	1 cold, chilly, lukewarm 2 calm, quiet, deliberate, distant, unfeeling, placid
correct	*adj*	right, proper, just, exact, accurate, true
	v	amend, admonish, punish, cure, reform
cost	*n*	price, charge, expense
costly	*adj*	dear, expensive, valuable
costume	*n*	dress, suit, robe, apparel, attire
count	*v*	1 number, reckon, score, calculate, enumerate, compute, estimate 2 matter 3 depend, rely, plan
couple	*n*	pair, two, brace, duet, partners
	v	join, link, tie, connect, unite, fasten
courage	*n*	bravery, boldness, heroism, pluck, valour, gallantry, daring
course	*n*	1 route, way, road, path, direction, track 2 method, plan, technique
courtesy	*n*	politeness, good manners, civility, consideration
cover	*v*	conceal, hide, shield, screen, shelter, disguise
crack	*v*	split, break, splinter, fracture
craft	*n*	art, skill, trade, cunning

Cc

crafty	*adj*	sly, cunning, artful, deceitful, wily, devious
cram	*v*	stuff, overfill, jam
crash	*n*	1 loud noise, bang, smash 2 collision, accident
crawl	*v*	creep, clamber
crazy	*adj*	foolish, silly, mad, nonsensical, insane, absurd
create	*v*	make, produce, design, invent, devise
creature	*n*	animal, beast, brute
credit	*v*	believe, accept
crew	*n*	gang, group, team, company, mob, band, crowd
crime	*n*	wrongdoing, offence
crisp	*adj*	brittle, crusty
criticize	*v*	find fault, complain about, censure
cross	*v* *adj*	1 travel across 2 oppose, defy angry, annoyed, upset, peevish, sulky
crowd	*n*	gathering, group, throng, mob, horde, multitude
cruel	*adj*	hurtful, spiteful, unkind, inhuman, vicious, brutal, savage, merciless, pitiless
crumble	*v*	break up, fall into pieces
crunch	*v*	crush, grind, squeeze
crush	*v*	1 crunch, grind, press, squeeze, squash, trample 2 overcome, subdue, defeat, beat, overwhelm, conquer
crust	*n*	rind, shell, covering, casing, coating
cry	*v*	1 shout, yell, call out, scream, shriek, exclaim 2 weep, sob, whine, whimper

cunning	*adj*	sly, crafty, artful, wily, deceitful, clever, skilful, devious, shrewd
curb	*v*	check, control, limit, keep back, bridle, restrict
cure	*v*	heal, make well, put right, remedy, correct, repair
curious	*adj*	1 inquisitive, prying 2 strange, odd, rare, unusual, queer, peculiar
current	*n* *adj*	flow, stream, course present, popular, common, general
curse	*v*	1 swear, blaspheme 2 damn, condemn
curve	*n*	bend, turn, arch, arc, graph
custom	*n*	habit, manner, fashion, practice, rule, tradition, usage
customer	*n*	buyer, purchaser, client
cut	*v*	divide, sever, wound, slit, slash, gash, clip, snip, open, puncture

Dd

dab	*n*	1 pat, gentle touch, tap 2 smear, small blob
daft	*adj*	silly, foolish, reckless, stupid, crazy, wild, brainless, ridiculous, absurd
daily	*adv*	every day, each day, often, frequently, constant
dainty	*adj*	neat, nice, delicate, pleasing, pretty, tasteful, small
damage	*v*	injure, hurt, harm, break, abuse, impair, mar, sabotage
damp	*v*	dampen, moisten, extinguish
danger	*n*	risk, peril, threat, menace, hazard
dare	*v*	1 attempt, venture, risk 2 challenge, defy, brave
daring	*adj*	bold, brave, adventurous, courageous, fearless, valiant, gallant, heroic
dark	*adj*	unlit, sunless, dim, dull, gloomy, drab, murky, dingy, shadowy, obscure, cheerless
darken	*v*	obscure, dim
darling	*n*	sweetheart, dearest, pet, idol, favourite, loved one, beloved
dart	*v* *n*	fly, spring, run, rush, dash, race, spurt arrow, missile
dash	*v*	run quickly, race, sprint, spurt, rush, dart
dawn	*n*	1 daybreak, break of day, sunrise 2 beginning, start, commencement, origin
daze	*v*	bewilder, confuse, stun, perplex
dazzle	*v* *n*	blind, confuse glare, blinding light, brightness
dead	*adj*	1 numb, dull, lifeless 2 not alive, deceased, extinct
deaden	*v*	numb, dull, lessen, soothe, freeze, soften, cushion, muffle, smother

deadly	*adj*	fatal, mortal, poisonous
deaf	*adj*	1 unable to hear 2 unwilling to listen, inattentive, heedless, unmindful
deal	*v*	1 handle, manage 2 trade, do business **deal out** give out, distribute
dealer	*n*	trader, merchant, shopkeeper, retailer, wholesaler
dear	*adj*	1 dearest, darling, beloved, cherished 2 not cheap, costly, expensive
decay	*v*	rot, wither, fade, waste away, spoil, rust, decline, deteriorate
deceitful	*adj*	cunning, sly, artful, false, double-dealing
deceive	*v*	cheat, swindle, mislead, trick, fool, bluff, hoax
decent	*adj*	1 proper, becoming, respectable, modest, not vulgar 2 satisfactory, passable, tolerable
decide	*v*	fix, arrange, settle, judge, determine, conclude, end
decision	*n*	conclusion, settlement, judgement
decorate	*v*	beautify, adorn, paint, furnish
decrease	*v*	lessen, reduce, lower, shrink, contract, diminish, drop, fall, soften, decline, depreciate
deed	*n*	act, action, feat, performance
defeat	*v*	beat, conquer, subdue, overcome, vanquish, rout, repulse
	n	failure, loss, downfall, rout
defend	*v*	protect, guard, support, uphold
definite	*adj*	exact, fixed, accurate, certain, sure, clear, distinct, precise
defy	*v*	1 dare, challenge, resist, oppose 2 ignore, disregard, flout

Dd

delay	*v*	1 postpone, hinder, defer 2 linger, loiter, dawdle, hesitate, wait
deliberate	*adj* *v*	intentional, considered think about, consider, consult
delicate	*adj*	1 fine, dainty 2 feeble, weak, frail, fragile, tender, sensitive
delicious	*adj*	tasty, sweet, enjoyable, pleasing, luscious, savoury, appetizing
delight	*v*	please, charm, thrill, make happy, enchant, entertain
deliver	*v*	hand over, bring, distribute
demand	*v*	ask, claim, request, apply for, urge, insist
den	*n*	nest, lair, retreat
dense	*adj*	thick, close, compact, solid, lush, concentrated
deny	*v*	1 contradict, repudiate 2 refuse, withhold
depart	*v*	1 leave, go out, go away, start out, withdraw, quit 2 diverge, deviate
depend	*v*	rely, trust
derelict	*adj*	forsaken, abandoned, deserted, neglected
descend	*v*	1 go down, drop, fall, sink 2 dismount, alight, settle
desert	*v* *n*	forsake, abandon, leave, vacate, neglect barren land, wilderness
deserted	*adj*	empty, vacant, forsaken, abandoned
deserve	*v*	earn, merit, win, be worthy of, be entitled

design	n	1 pattern, decoration, sketch, drawing 2 object, plan, aim, intention, scheme, idea, purpose
desire	v	want, wish for, crave
desolate	adj	1 lone, alone, forlorn, unhappy, solitary, sad, wretched, miserable 2 lonely, deserted, forsaken, uninhabited
desperate	adj	1 rash, reckless, bold, wild, savage, violent, frantic 2 hopeless, not promising
despise	v	scorn, treat with contempt, dislike
destroy	v	finish, wreck, ruin, pull down, smash, demolish, spoil, kill
detain	v	hold, arrest, keep waiting, delay, hinder
detect	v	find, discover, perceive, notice
determine	v	decide, arrange, find out, learn, settle, estimate, resolve
determined	adj	1 firm, resolute, dogged, persevering, unwavering, unflinching 2 resolved, decided, settled
detest	v	hate, dislike, abhor, loathe
develop	v	improve, expand, increase, enlarge, extend, grow
devoted	adj	loyal, faithful, true, constant, earnest, sincere, dedicated
devour	v	consume, eat greedily, swallow
die	v	expire, pass away, wither, fade, perish
different	adj	1 not alike, unlike, dissimilar 2 unusual, uncommon, special, novel
difficulty	n	problem, obstacle, bother, trouble, burden, hardship, plight, dilemma, predicament
dignity	n	pride, eminence, worthiness, grandeur

Dd

dim	*adj*	dull, faint, indistinct, dark, vague, obscure
dingy	*adj*	shabby, faded, grimy, dirty, squalid
dip	*n*	1 dive, immersion 2 swim, bath 3 hollow, incline, depression
direct	*adj*	1 straight, short, express, abrupt 2 outspoken, straightforward, frank
	v	1 govern, manage, control, order, guide, conduct 2 address, send, aim
direction	*n*	1 way, route, path, aim, course 2 order, rule, instruction, command
directly	*adv*	quickly, promptly, soon, presently, immediately
dirty	*adj*	muddy, dusty, filthy, foul, grimy, unclean, unwashed, impure, soiled, sooty, smudged, stained, tarnished, sordid
disagree	*v*	differ, argue, quarrel
disappear	*v*	vanish, become invisible
disaster	*n*	catastrophe, tragedy, mishap, calamity, misfortune
discuss	*v*	debate, talk over, argue, consider
disgrace	*v*	put to shame, dishonour, degrade
disguise	*v*	hide, conceal, mask, cover up, veil, camouflage, misrepresent
disgusting	*adj*	nasty, revolting, loathsome, repulsive
dismal	*adj*	dreary, drab, cheerless, dingy, sad, miserable, gloomy, mournful, depressing, dull
display	*n*	show, exhibition, demonstration, parade, pageant
	v	show, exhibit, parade, demonstrate
displease	*v*	offend, vex, annoy, make indignant, irritate
distant	*adj*	1 far away, remote, at a distance 2 cold, shy, reserved, cool

distasteful	adj	nasty, unappetizing, disagreeable, disgusting, objectionable
distinct	adj	1 clear, plain, obvious, definite, unmistakable 2 separate, different, individual
distress	n	trouble, grief, worry, concern, anxiety, sadness, misery, discomfort, sorrow, anguish
distrust	n	doubt, disbelief, suspicion, mistrust
disturb	v	bother, worry, pester, annoy, agitate, upset, unsettle, irritate
divide	v	separate, cut, part, sever, break, share, distribute, deal
do	v	make, act, perform, operate, achieve
dodge	v	avoid, move aside, duck, sidestep, elude, evade
doubtful	adj	uncertain, unsure, undecided, vague, indefinite, dubious, unsettled, questionable, hesitating
doubtless	adv	without a doubt, certainly, surely, definitely, decidedly, unquestionably
drab	adj	dull, dreary, shabby, gloomy, plain, monotonous
drag	v	1 pull, haul, tow, tug, draw 2 dredge, search
drain	v n	empty, exhaust gutter, outlet, channel, trench, conduit, sewer, ditch
drastic	adj	violent, vigorous, ruthless
draw	v	1 attract, pull, haul, tow, tug, drag, extract 2 sketch, design
dreadful	adj	fearful, alarming, terrible, awful, horrible, dire, horrid
dream	n	fancy, vision, trance, nightmare
dreary	adj	drab, dull, barren, cheerless, dingy, gloomy, boring, tedious, dismal

Dd

dress	*n*	clothes, clothing, garments, apparel, attire, costume, robes
drift	*v*	wander, float
drive	*v*	1 guide, steer, control, direct, pilot 2 press, make, persuade, compel, urge, force
drop	*n*	1 fall, descent, dive 2 tiny quantity, globule, bead
	v	let go, leave, abandon
drown	*v*	1 flood, drench, soak 2 stifle, suffocate, extinguish, muffle, deaden
drowsy	*adj*	sleepy, sluggish, languid, dozy
dry	*adj*	1 without water, waterless, rainless, arid 2 thirsty, parched 3 dull, boring, uninteresting, tedious
dull	*adj*	1 dim, drab, faint, obscure, not bright, cloudy, sunless 2 stupid, backward, dense, uninteresting
dusk	*n*	shade, gloom, semi-darkness, twilight, nightfall
duty	*n*	1 obligation, service, work, office 2 tax payment
dwell	*v*	live, reside, abide, lodge
dwindle	*v*	lessen, reduce, diminish, decrease, shrink, decline
dye	*n*	paint, pigment, colour, stain

eager	*adj*	keen, willing, earnest, zealous, determined, enthusiastic, ardent
early	*adv*	beforehand, before time, in advance
	adj	long ago, former
earn	*v*	gain, obtain, work for, merit, win, deserve, attain, achieve
earnest	*adj*	serious, keen, willing, sincere, eager, determined, conscientious
ease	*n*	rest, calm, comfort, leisure, relaxation
	v	reduce, lessen, relieve, soothe, relax, adjust
easy	*adj*	restful, relaxed, calm, comfortable, leisurely, effortless, simple, not difficult
eat	*v*	1 dine, consume, feed on, devour 2 wear away, rust, corrode, erode
edge	*n*	margin, boundary, border, verge, rim, brink, brim
educate	*v*	teach, instruct, train, guide, inform
eerie	*adj*	strange, weird, ghostly
effect	*n*	result, outcome, consequence
	v	do, complete, accomplish
effective	*adj*	1 able, efficient 2 striking, pleasing, attractive, impressive
efficient	*adj*	able, effective, skilful, capable, businesslike, competent
effort	*n*	1 attempt, try, endeavour, struggle 2 work, labour, toil, exertion, energy, action
elastic	*adj*	springy, supple, flexible
elated	*adj*	excited, merry, gleeful, joyful, overjoyed, overcome
elegant	*adj*	graceful, beautiful, handsome, dignified, stylish, tasteful, refined
elementary	*adj*	simple, easy, basic
else	*adv*	otherwise, if not, besides

Ee

embark	*v*	1 board, go aboard, go on board 2 start, begin, set out
emblem	*n*	badge, mark, sign, crest, symbol, device
embrace	*v*	1 hug, clasp, hold 2 include, contain, enclose
emerge	*v*	come into view, appear, arise
emergency	*n*	urgency, difficulty, crisis
emphasize	*v*	stress, draw attention to
employ	*v*	give work to, engage, hire, appoint, occupy
empty	*v* *adj*	pour out, drain, evacuate vacant, unoccupied, barren, deserted, bare
enchant	*v*	charm, delight, please, fascinate, bewitch, entrance
enclose	*v*	contain, surround, envelop, conceal, wrap
encounter	*v*	meet, confront
encourage	*v*	give support to, inspire, assure, hearten, cheer, comfort
end	*v* *n*	finish, cease, halt, stop, complete, conclude, destroy, close 1 aim, object, intention, result, outcome, purpose 2 tip, point, extremity
endless	*adj*	boundless, everlasting, eternal, continual, continuous, ceaseless, perpetual, uninterrupted, unending, incessant
endure	*v*	1 put up with, bear, suffer, accept, undergo, submit to, tolerate 2 last, exist, live, remain, continue
enemy	*n*	foe, adversary, opponent
energetic	*adj*	active, vigorous, brisk, lively, alive, forceful
energy	*n*	vigour, power, force, zest, stamina, enthusiasm, activity

engage	*v*	1 employ, hire, find work for, appoint 2 undertake, promise, pledge
enjoyment	*n*	pleasure, delight, amusement, happiness
enlarge	*v*	make larger, increase, expand, extend, magnify, widen
enormous	*adj*	gigantic, huge, colossal, tremendous, vast, immense
enough	*adj*	ample, sufficient, plenty
enquire (inquire)	*v*	ask, question, investigate
enter	*v*	go into, invade, encroach, penetrate
entertain	*v*	1 amuse, delight, divert, occupy, please 2 consider, welcome
enthusiasm	*n*	keenness, eagerness, zeal, zest, willingness, determination
entice	*v*	tempt, attract, coax, persuade, lure
entire	*adj*	complete, whole, full, total
entrance	*n*	entry, inlet, access, opening, doorway, gateway, passage
envy	*v*	jealousy
episode	*n*	incident, event, occasion
equal	*adj*	alike, the same, equivalent, even, uniform, balanced, identical
equip	*v*	supply, provide, fit out, furnish
equivalent	*adj*	alike, the same, equal, corresponding
erect	*v* *adj*	build, construct, raise, put up upright, vertical, perpendicular
error	*n*	mistake, fault, blunder, oversight
erupt	*v*	burst out, blow up, explode, eject

Ee

escape	*v*	1 become free, leak, take flight, flee, make off, steal away, get away, abscond 2 avoid, evade, dodge, flee
essential	*adj*	necessary, needed, requisite, vital, very important
estimate	*v*	judge, measure, gauge, approximate, compute, reckon, count, calculate
eternal	*adj*	everlasting, perpetual, endless, abiding, unchanging
even	*adj*	level, flat, smooth, regular, exact, uniform
event	*n*	incident, happening, episode, affair, occasion
eventually	*adv*	at last, in time, finally
everlasting	*adj*	eternal, perpetual, endless, abiding, continual, ceaseless
evil	*adj*	wicked, sinful, corrupt, vicious, immoral, unpleasant
exact	*adj*	just, true, correct, definite, accurate, precise
examine	*v*	check, test, inspect, look at, search, investigate, observe, study
example	*n*	specimen, model, sample, pattern, copy
exceed	*v*	be larger than, be greater than, go beyond, overstep
excel	*v*	do well, beat, surpass, eclipse
excellent	*adj*	outstanding, superior, perfect, superb, choice
exceptional	*adj*	outstanding, special, rare, unusual, uncommon, extraordinary, abnormal
excess	*n*	surplus, abundance
excite	*v*	arouse, enliven, stir, agitate, awaken
excursion	*n*	trip, outing, journey, expedition, tour, ramble

excuse	*v*	pardon, overlook, forgive, exempt
exercise	*n*	task, activity, drill
exhausted	*adj*	1 tired, weary, fatigued, weakened 2 used up, consumed, drained away
exist	*v*	live, survive
exit	*n* *v*	way out, departure go out, leave, depart
expand	*v*	increase, enlarge, swell, extend, stretch, spread, magnify, unfold
expect	*v*	wait for, look forward to, anticipate
expensive	*adj*	dear, costly, high-priced
expert	*adj*	skilful, talented, clever, well-trained, experienced
explain	*v*	make clear, show, illustrate
exploit	*n*	deed, adventure, escapade, feat, stunt, achievement
explore	*v*	search, look at, examine, investigate
expose	*v*	uncover, bare, show, display
express	*adj* *v*	1 quick, fast, rapid, speedy, swift, without delay 2 definite, exact, clear state, declare, show, utter
expression	*n*	1 statement, remark, declaration 2 look, show, appearance
extend	*v*	stretch, lengthen, increase, spread, enlarge, prolong
exterior	*adj*	outside, outer, outward, external
extra	*adj*	surplus, spare, additional
extract	*v* *n*	pull out, remove, withdraw, copy quotation, passage (from a book), section, selection
extraordinary	*adj*	strange, uncommon, unusual, special, rare, surprising, incredible, amazing, astounding, astonishing, remarkable

Ee

extravagance	*n*	needless waste, foolish spending, excess
extreme	*adj*	farthest, utmost, most distant
extremely	*adv*	exceedingly, exceptionally
eye	*v*	look at, observe, watch, gaze
eye-opener	*n*	surprise, shock

fab	*adj*	fabulous, wonderful, marvellous, splendid, superb, delightful
fable	*n*	story, tale, legend, myth
fabulous	*adj*	legendary, fanciful, astounding, extraordinary, wonderful, splendid, incredible
face	*n*	1 countenance, visage 2 front, outside, exterior, surface
	v	meet, confront, oppose
fade	*v*	become faint, grow dim, lose colour, wither, droop, wane
fail	*v*	1 miss, neglect, be unsuccessful 2 let down, disappoint 3 weaken, become feeble
faint	*v* *adj*	swoon, droop, weaken 1 weak, feeble, exhausted, sluggish 2 not clear, dim, indistinct, vague, faded, pale, dull
fair	*adj*	1 just right, correct, proper, honest 2 handsome, beautiful, attractive 3 bright, clear, fine, sunny 4 average, passable
faith	*n*	belief, trust, confidence, assurance
faithful	*adj*	loyal, true, trustworthy, constant, devoted, conscientious, reliable
fake	*adj*	sham, false, fraudulent, forged, imitation
fall	*v*	1 drop, descend, plunge, tumble, go down 2 lower, lessen, diminish, decrease
false	*adj*	1 sham, imitation, fake, forged, fraudulent, make-believe 2 untrue, incorrect, wrong, mistaken 3 disloyal, unfaithful, deceitful
fame	*n*	renown, reputation, greatness, honour
familiar	*adj*	1 well-known, common, everyday, commonplace, ordinary 2 friendly, sociable, kindly, courteous
family	*n*	folk, relations, relatives, household

Ff

famous	*adj*	great, famed, celebrated, well-known, noted, renowned, distinguished
fancy	*n*	idea, belief, whim, fantasy, imagination
	adj	decorated, ornamental
fantastic	*adj*	fanciful, imagined, fabulous, unreal, far-fetched, unusual
far	*adj*	distant, remote, far-away
far-fetched	*adj*	exaggerated, unbelievable
fare	*v*	go, live, manage, turn out
	n	1 payment, charge (for a journey) 2 food, provisions
farming	*n*	agriculture, cultivation
farther	*adj*	more distant/remote/advanced
	adv	at a greater distance
fascinate	*v*	charm, attract, entice, enchant, delight
fashion	*v*	shape, mould, design, make, create
	n	style, manner, way, custom, tradition
fast	*adj*	1 quick, rapid, swift, speedy, fleet, brisk 2 fixed, tight, secure, fastened
	v	hunger, go without food
fasten	*v*	fix, attach, tie, knot, join, connect, secure
fat	*n*	grease, oil
	adj	plump, stout, gross
fatal	*adj*	deadly, ruinous, mortal
fate	*n*	fortune, luck, lot, destiny, doom
fatigue	*v*	tire, weary, weaken, exhaust
fault	*n*	error, mistake, defect, flaw, failing, weakness
favour	*v*	please, be kind to, prefer, approve
favourable	*adj*	helpful, useful, hopeful, promising, kind, approving, beneficial
fear	*n*	dread, terror, fright, alarm, cowardice, anxiety, panic

fearless	*adj*	bold, brave, courageous, gallant, daring, valiant, heroic
feast	*n*	1 meal, banquet 2 festival, fête, holiday, anniversary
feat	*n*	act, deed, exploit, achievement
feeble	*adj*	weak, delicate, frail, exhausted, infirm, sickly
feel	*v*	1 touch, handle, grope 2 be moved/affected/excited
feeling	*n*	touch, sensation, emotion
feminine	*adj*	female, womanly, ladylike, tender, delicate
fence	*n* *v*	barrier, railing, barricade 1 enclose 2 evade, avoid, parry, hedge
ferocious	*adj*	fierce, savage, wild, cruel, untamed
fertile	*adj*	rich, fruitful, cultivated, productive
fetch	*v*	bring, carry, obtain, get, transport
fever	*n*	1 illness, sickness, disease 2 eagerness, excitement, passion
fib	*n* *v*	lie, untruth, falsehood lie, mislead
fidget	*v*	fret, fuss, toss and turn, twitch
fierce	*adj*	ferocious, savage, wild, violent
fight	*n*	struggle, combat, battle, contest, conflict, action, engagement
figure	*n*	1 shape, outline, pattern, form, body 2 digit, number, symbol, numeral
fill	*v*	pack, store, stuff, put in, pour in
final	*adj*	end, last, concluding, decisive
find	*v*	discover, search for, look for, detect, recover, solve
fine	*adj*	1 thin, delicate, slender 2 handsome, choice, best, excellent, of quality 3 dry, sunny, bright

Ff

finish	*v*	end, close, complete, conclude
firm	*adj*	fixed, steady, hard, tight, secure, determined, steadfast, solid
first	*adv*	earliest, initial
fit	*v*	agree with, suit, match
	n	seizure, spasm, bout, whim, attack
	adj	1 well, healthy 2 proper, suitable, right
fix	*v*	1 fasten, join, attach, secure, connect 2 mend, repair, adjust 3 decide, arrange, settle, organize
	n	problem, difficulty, plight
flabby	*adj*	limp, slack, soft, loose, fleshy, yielding
flame	*v*	blaze, flare, burn
flash	*n*	1 gleam, glow, flare, sparkle 2 moment, second, twinkling, instant
flat	*adj*	1 level, even, smooth, horizontal 2 tasteless, stale, dull, uninteresting
flavour	*n*	taste, relish, savour
flee	*v*	run away, escape, fly, abscond
flicker	*v*	flutter, quiver, shake, twitch, shimmer, flash, vibrate
flight	*n*	1 escape, rapid departure 2 glide, journey by air, migration **flight of steps** stairs, stairway, staircase
fling	*v*	hurl, throw, cast, toss, heave, pitch
float	*v*	drift, hover
flow	*v*	pour out, stream, gush, run, flood
fluster	*v*	upset, confuse, fuss, bother, agitate
fly	*v*	1 flee, escape, abscond 2 soar, wing, glide, hover
foggy	*adj*	misty, cloudy, blurred, hazy, vague, dim, unclear

folk	*n*	people, persons, relations, relatives, nation, race
follow	*v*	1 hunt, go after, chase, pursue, track 2 copy, imitate 3 result from 4 grasp, understand
fond	*adj*	affectionate, loving, caring, devoted, tender
food	*n*	fare, nourishment, provisions, rations
fool	*n*	idiot, clown, buffoon, oaf, jester, simpleton
	v	1 joke, play, clown, jest 2 deceive, hoodwink, trick, bluff, cheat
foolhardy	*adj*	reckless, rash, headstrong, thoughtless
foot	*n*	base, bottom
forbid	*v*	not allow, not permit, ban, prevent, prohibit
force	*v*	make, drive, compel
	n	strength, power, might, energy, effort
forecast	*v*	foresee, foretell, predict, prophesy, divine, estimate, anticipate
foreign	*adj*	1 alien, from another land 2 strange, unknown
forget	*v*	not remember, overlook, neglect
forgive	*v*	pardon, excuse, acquit, overlook
forlorn	*adj*	lonely, friendless, forsaken, neglected, dejected, downcast, unhappy, sad, miserable, wretched
form	*n*	shape, outline, figure, body
former	*adj*	earlier, previous, preceding
forsake	*v*	desert, abandon, leave, vacate, renounce, depart from
fortunate	*adj*	lucky, favoured, successful, prosperous

Ff

fortune	*n*	1 luck, fate, lot, destiny, chance 2 wealth, riches, prosperity
foul	*adj*	1 unfair, nasty, unpleasant, vulgar, obscene 2 unclean, filthy, soiled, dirty, tainted
foundation	*n*	bottom, base, footing, basis
fraction	*n*	part, portion, piece, bit, section, division, fragment
fracture	*v*	break, snap, crack, split
fragile	*adj*	breakable, flimsy, weak, delicate, brittle, frail
fragment	*n*	small piece, bit, morsel, scrap, chip, splinter
frantic	*adj*	desperate, frenzied, very excited, crazy, panicky, uncontrolled
free	*adj*	1 liberated, at liberty, loose, independent 2 open, frank, candid, sincere 3 generous, liberal 4 at no charge, gratis
frequent	*adj*	repeated, regular, many, numerous
fresh	*adj*	1 new, recent, different, novel 2 brisk, lively, bracing, refreshing
fret	*v*	worry, bother, fuss, grieve
friend	*n*	chum, mate, pal, companion, comrade
friendly	*adj*	kind, genial, amiable, sociable, affectionate
frighten	*v*	scare, alarm, make afraid, terrify, shock
frightful	*adj*	dreadful, terrible, awful, shocking, alarming, horrid, hideous, fearful
front	*n*	face, foremost part, outside
frown	*v*	scowl, look sour **frown upon** disapprove of

fruitful	*adj*	fertile, rich, abundant, productive
fulfil	*v*	complete, carry out, accomplish
full	*adj*	1 complete, whole, entire, perfect 2 filled, containing
fun	*n*	amusement, merriment, play, sport, gaiety, jollity, frolic
funny	*adj*	1 amusing, comical, laughable, humorous 2 peculiar, queer, odd, strange
furious	*adj*	angry, enraged, wild, mad, frantic, very annoyed, wrathful, infuriated
further	*adv* *adj*	farther, more distant additional, extra
fury	*n*	rage, anger, ferocity, frenzy
fuss	*v*	bother, worry, fidget, fret, agitate

Gg

gag	*n*	joke, trick, hoax
	v	silence, muffle
gain	*v*	obtain, receive, win, collect, acquire
gallant	*adj*	brave, bold, daring, dashing, courageous, heroic, fearless
game	*n*	sport, play, amusement, fun, contest, match, pastime
	adj	brave, bold, daring, willing
gang	*n*	crew, group, company, crowd, band
gaol	*n*	prison, penitentiary, cell, dungeon, jail
gap	*n*	hole, space, blank, opening, interval
garments	*n*	items of dress, clothes, clothing, apparel
gasp	*v*	gulp, pant, puff, blow
gather	*v*	1 collect, pick up, cull, crop, harvest, pluck 2 meet, assemble, congregate
gaudy	*adj*	showy, flashy, glossy
gaunt	*adj*	lean, haggard, grim, thin
gay	*adj*	joyful, joyous, happy, jolly, cheerful, merry, light-hearted, gleeful, lively
gear	*n*	equipment, tools, tackle, property, apparatus, equipment
gem	*n*	jewel, precious stone
general	*adj*	common, usual, ordinary, normal, customary, widespread, prevalent
generous	*adj*	1 not mean, freely-giving, liberal 2 ample, abundant, plentiful
genial	*adj*	cordial, friendly, jovial, pleasant, kindly, cheerful, sociable, agreeable
gentle	*adj*	1 soft, tender, light, mild, kind, quiet, tame, timid 2 genteel, well-born, honourable
genuine	*adj*	real, true, sound, straight, sincere, authentic

get	*v*	obtain, receive, win, acquire, borrow, collect, achieve, pick, catch, select, choose, take, arrive, secure
ghastly	*adj*	pale, white, wan, ghostlike, weird, unearthly, death-like, horrible, frightful, dreadful, terrible, shocking, gruesome, hideous
ghost	*n*	spirit, phantom, spectre, apparition
giant	*adj*	gigantic, very large, great, huge, immense, enormous, tremendous, colossal
giddy	*adj*	1 dizzy, dazed, faint, unsteady 2 excitable, frivolous
gift	*n*	1 present, donation, grant, contribution, subscription, bounty 2 talent, virtue, ability, power
gigantic	*adj*	giant, very large, great, huge, immense, enormous, massive, vast, tremendous, colossal
give	*v*	1 present, grant, award, allow, hand over, provide, donate 2 collapse, break, bend
glad	*adj*	pleased, pleasing, happy, contented, delighted, joyful, joyous, cheerful
glamorous	*adj*	beautiful, pretty, attractive, bewitching, charming
glance	*n* *v*	quick look, glimpse bounce, ricochet
glare	*n*	1 dazzle, gleam, flash, glow, glitter 2 angry look, stare
gleam	*n*	light, flash, beam, glow, glare
glimpse	*n*	glance, quick look
glisten	*v*	shine, glitter, gleam, flash, sparkle, twinkle, shimmer
globe	*n*	ball, orb, sphere
gloomy	*adj*	sad, cheerless, dull, glum, depressed, unhappy, dismal, downcast, dejected, melancholy, mournful, sullen, dark, dreary, drab, pessimistic

Gg

glorious   *adj*   splendid, magnificent, delightful, brilliant, radiant

glossy   *adj*   shiny, gleaming, flashy, gaudy

glue   *n*   gum, paste, adhesive, fixative

glum   *adj*   sad, unhappy, dismal, gloomy, melancholy, downcast, dejected, pessimistic, sullen, moody

go   *v*
1 move, start, leave, depart
2 journey, travel, proceed
3 pass, elapse
4 move, act, operate

     n   turn, opportunity

goal   *n*   aim, object, purpose, ambition, target

good   *adj*
1 true, right, just, kind, gentle, saintly, worthy, virtuous, upright, well-behaved, righteous, generous
2 favourable, beneficial, helpful, fine, nice, superior, sound, wholesome, reliable, profitable, fresh, pure
3 skilful, talented, clever

goods   *n*
1 merchandise, wares
2 possessions, belongings

gorge   *n*   pass, canyon, ravine
     v   eat greedily, devour, bolt

gorgeous   *adj*   magnificent, splendid, ornate, lovely, dazzling

gossip   *v*   talk idly, chatter, prattle

govern   *v*   control, rule, manage, conduct, guide, direct, command, lead, sway, determine, decide

grab   *v*   seize, snatch, clutch, grip, clasp, hold, grasp, capture

graceful   *adj*   elegant, refined, charming, attractive, beautiful

gracious   *adj*   polite, courteous, well-mannered, kind, agreeable, charming, graceful

gradually   *adv*   slowly, cautiously, by degrees

grand   *adj*   great, big, large, immense, fine, magnificent, splendid, superb, stately, dignified, important

grant	*v*	give, present, award, provide, allow, permit
grasp	*v*	1 seize, grab, clutch, clasp, grip, hold, capture 2 know, understand
grateful	*adj*	thankful, appreciative
gravely	*adv*	sternly, severely, seriously, solemnly
great	*adj*	1 big, large, grand, huge, vast, immense, gigantic, important, famous, majestic, powerful, celebrated 2 marvellous, wonderful
greedy	*adj*	covetous, grasping, gluttonous, avaricious, selfish
greet	*v*	welcome, hail, salute, bid, acknowledge
grey	*adj*	dull, leaden, dismal
grief	*n*	1 sorrow, distress, sadness, woe, misery, heartache, regret, anguish, mourning 2 misfortune, failure, disaster
grip	*v*	clutch, grasp, hold, clasp, seize, grab, capture
groan	*v*	moan, cry with pain, whimper, complain, grumble
grope	*v*	feel, search
gross	*adj*	1 big, large, great, bulky, fat, bloated, overfed 2 glaring, flagrant, outrageous 3 total, whole, entire
ground	*n*	earth, floor, base
group	*n*	1 set, collection, class, cluster, number, quantity, classification 2 crowd, company, gang, crew, knot
grow	*v*	1 become bigger, enlarge, increase, extend, expand, swell, stretch, develop, spread 2 shoot, sprout, cultivate, multiply, germinate, raise

Gg

growl	*v*	snarl, mutter, grumble, complain, murmur
grown-up	*adj*	grown, adult, mature
gruesome	*adj*	ghastly, horrible, horrifying, frightening, dreadful, hideous, ugly, grisly, repulsive, revolting
gruff	*adj*	harsh, stern, surly, churlish
grumble	*v*	complain, groan, murmur, object
guard	*v*	protect, defend
guess	*v*	suppose, suspect, imagine, estimate
guest	*n*	visitor, lodger, boarder
guide	*v*	lead, direct, conduct, advise
guile	*n*	deceit, treachery, trickery, cunning, slyness, artfulness, fraud
gum	*n*	glue, paste, adhesive
gun	*n*	weapon, firearm, pistol, revolver, cannon, rifle
gush	*v*	rush out, stream, flow quickly
gust	*n*	wind, breeze, blast, squall

habit	*n*	custom, tradition, practice, rule, routine, procedure, manner
haggard	*adj*	careworn, worn out, gaunt, drawn, tired, weary, lean, worn
hail	*v*	greet, salute, signal, call, shout, acknowledge, welcome
halt	*v*	stop, arrest, hesitate, pause, rest, wait
hammer	*v*	hit, beat, rap, tap, knock, strike, drive, bang
handicap	*n*	disadvantage, disability, hindrance, burden, obstruction
	v	hinder, hamper, impede, obstruct
handle	*v*	1 hold, touch, feel 2 deal with, control, manage, use
handsome	*adj*	fair, good-looking, beautiful, lovely, pretty, comely, graceful, elegant
handy	*adj*	1 near, close by, within reach, useful, helpful, convenient 2 skilful, skilled, clever
hang	*v*	suspend, drape, droop, dangle, swing
haphazard	*adj*	jumbled, at random, by chance, unplanned
happen	*v*	occur, come to pass, take place, chance, befall
happy	*adj*	contented, delighted, joyful, joyous, glad, pleased, cheerful, cheery, jolly, jovial, merry, gleeful, gay, carefree, blithe, light-hearted, smiling, satisfied
harass	*v*	pester, plague, annoy, trouble, bother, worry, vex, torment, molest
hard	*adj*	1 firm, solid, rigid, stiff 2 stern, severe, harsh, unfeeling, pitiless, unkind, cruel 3 not easy, difficult
hardly	*adv*	scarcely, barely, only just, not quite
hardship	*n*	misfortune, mishap, trouble, trial, difficulty, burden, handicap
hardy	*adj*	strong, sturdy, hearty, robust, vigorous

Hh

harm	*v*	hurt, injure, damage, wrong, abuse
harmless	*adj*	not harmful, innocent, not damaging
harsh	*adj*	1 rough, severe, strict, hard, unfeeling, unkind, pitiless, cruel 2 grating, jarring, unpleasant, unmusical
harvest	*n* *v*	crop, produce collect, gather, pick, reap
hasty	*adj*	1 quick, fast, rapid, swift, speedy, brisk 2 abrupt, reckless, rash, hurried, thoughtless
hate	*v*	dislike, loathe, detest, despise
haughty	*adj*	proud, vain, snobbish, arrogant
haul	*v*	pull, draw, drag, tow
have	*v*	possess, hold, own, obtain **have to** ought, must, should
hazard	*n*	risk, danger, peril, menace
hazy	*adj*	1 misty, cloudy, foggy, dim, dull, indistinct 2 doubtful, vague, not clear, uncertain, indefinite, confused
head	*n*	1 chief, principal, leader 2 top, upper end, source, summit 3 mind, brain, intelligence
headlong	*adv*	1 headfirst 2 hastily, rashly, recklessly
headstrong	*adj*	stubborn, obstinate, rash, reckless, wilful, hot-headed
heal	*v*	cure, restore, remedy, treat
healthy	*adj*	well, fit, sound, robust, vigorous
heap	*n*	pile, mound, stack, mass
heart	*n*	centre, middle, core, kernel

hH

heartless	*adj*	unfeeling, uncaring, pitiless, cruel, unkind, callous, brutal
hearty	*adj*	1 friendly, cordial, good-natured, cheerful, jovial, genial, sincere 2 strong, sturdy, robust, healthy, sound
heat	*n*	1 hotness, warmth, glow 2 anger, fury, annoyance 3 excitement, zeal, passion
heavy	*adj*	weighty, massive, abundant
hectic	*adj*	feverish, exciting, bustling, busy
heed	*v*	notice, regard, observe, mind
hefty	*adj*	heavy, big, large, strong, sturdy
help	*v*	aid, assist, support
heroic	*adj*	brave, bold, courageous, valiant, gallant, noble
hesitate	*v*	pause, waver, falter, delay
hide	*v*	conceal, keep secret, cover, lurk, disguise, bury, suppress
	n	skin, pelt
hideous	*adj*	ugly, horrible, horrid, frightful, repulsive
high	*adj*	1 tall, steep, lofty, raised, topmost 2 eminent, important, chief, superior 3 strong, shrill, keen, acute
hill	*n*	mount, mound, hillock, slope
hinder	*v*	hamper, delay, check, block, impede, obstruct, prevent
hint	*n*	suggestion, clue, inkling, indication
hire	*v*	employ, engage, set on
hit	*v*	strike, beat, punch, thump, slap, clout, rap, tap, knock, hit, cuff
hitch	*v*	fasten, tie up, tether, attach
	n	difficulty, problem, hindrance, delay

Hh

hoard	*n*	hidden store, stockpile, collection, cache
	v	collect, stock, store
hoarse	*adj*	husky, gruff, harsh, croaking
hoax	*v*	trick, fool, deceive, cheat
hold	*v*	1 grasp, grab, clasp, seize, stop, arrest, grip 2 have, own, possess, keep, retain 3 believe, declare, consider
hole	*n*	hollow, pit, cavity, space, excavation
holiday	*n*	vacation, rest, leave, festival
hollow	*adj*	1 empty, not solid, sunken 2 shallow, insincere, deceitful
	n	hole, pit, cavity, dell, valley
holy	*adj*	sacred, godly, revered, blessed, divine, consecrated
home	*n*	dwelling, residence, abode
homely	*adj*	plain, simple, ordinary, coarse, commonplace, homespun
honest	*adj*	true, upright, straight, open, fair, straightforward, truthful, sincere, trustworthy, just
honour	*n*	good reputation, respect, esteem
hoodwink	*v*	cheat, trick, deceive, fool, dupe
hope	*v*	wish, expect, anticipate, desire
hopeless	*adj*	without hope, desperate, impossible
horrible	*adj*	horrid, terrible, dreadful, hideous, awful, frightful, shocking
horrify	*v*	frighten, shock, alarm, fill with dread, terrify
host	*n*	1 large crowd, army, multitude 2 hotel-keeper, landlord
hostile	*adj*	unfriendly, threatening, warlike
hot	*adj*	1 very warm, burning, glowing, fiery, boiling, heated, sunny, tropical 2 eager, hasty, quick

house	*n*	dwelling, shelter, abode, residence
however	*adv*	but, still, nevertheless
	conj	but, nevertheless
hug	*v*	clasp, embrace, squeeze
huge	*adj*	large, big, great, giant, gigantic, enormous, vast, bulky, immense, colossal
humane	*adj*	kind, merciful, tender, sympathetic
humble	*adj*	meek, modest, unassuming, lowly
humour	*n*	1 amusement, fun, comedy 2 whim, fancy, mood
	v	pamper, spoil, agree with, indulge
hungry	*adj*	starving, famished, ravenous
hunt	*v*	search, seek, trace, chase, pursue, follow, track, trail
hurl	*v*	throw, fling, heave, toss, pitch, sling, cast
hurry	*v*	haste, hasten, speed, rush, scurry, dash
hurt	*v*	injure, harm, pain, wound, maim, offend, damage

Ii

icy	*adj*	1 frozen, frosty, cold 2 unfriendly, distant, cool
idea	*n*	thought, fancy, plan, scheme, design, notion
ideal	*adj*	perfect, faultless
idiotic	*adj*	stupid, foolish, silly, absurd, crazy, ridiculous
idle	*adj*	1 lazy, sluggish, inactive, slack, motionless 2 empty, vain, useless 3 barren, unused
ignite	*v*	set alight, light, take fire, burn
ignorant	*adj*	without knowledge, uneducated, illiterate, uninformed
ignore	*v*	refuse to notice, disregard
ill	*adj*	1 sick, unwell, ailing 2 bad, evil 3 unlucky, unfortunate
illness	*n*	sickness, ill health, poor health
illuminate	*v*	light, light up, shine upon, brighten
imaginary	*adj*	unreal, fanciful, fancied, supposed, pretended, make believe
imagine	*v*	suppose, pretend, fancy, make believe, assume
imitate	*v*	copy, watch, follow, mimic
immediately	*adv*	now, at this time, promptly, at once, without delay, instantly, right away, this instant, directly
immense	*adj*	very large, great, enormous, huge, giant, gigantic, vast, tremendous, colossal
immortal	*adj*	undying, abiding, everlasting, eternal, divine, constant
impatient	*adj*	restless, fidgety, fretful, fussy, eager, intolerant
imperfect	*adj*	incomplete, faulty, defective, tainted, damaged

impertinent	*adj*	cheeky, rude, forward, impudent, impolite, insolent
implore	*v*	beg, beseech, entreat, pray
impolite	*adj*	rude, discourteous, uncivil, cheeky, bad-mannered, ill-mannered, disrespectful, impertinent
important	*adj*	1 essential, urgent, vital, pressing 2 famous, notable, celebrated
improper	*adj*	not proper, incorrect, wrong, unseemly, indecent
impudent	*adj*	cheeky, insolent, rude, impertinent, forward, disrespectful
impure	*adj*	tainted, foul, dirty, unclean, polluted
incident	*n*	event, happening, affair, episode, occurrence
incorrect	*adj*	wrong, faulty, unsuitable, untrue, inaccurate, improper
increase	*v*	make larger, enlarge, grow, gain, expand, raise, multiply
indeed	*adv*	in truth, really, truly, certainly
indefinite	*adj*	uncertain, unsure, undecided, vague, unlimited
indicate	*v*	point out, show, mark, tell, suggest
indignant	*adj*	resentful, annoyed, angry, scornful
indistinct	*adj*	dim, blurred, obscure, vague, faint
individual	*adj*	single, particular, special
industrious	*adj*	busy, hard-working, very active, diligent
inferior	*adj*	1 lower, below 2 poor, second-rate, mediocre
infirm	*adj*	feeble, frail, weak, ailing
influence	*v*	affect, sway, persuade, direct
inform	*v*	tell, make known to, advise, instruct, notify
infrequent	*adj*	not often, rare, occasional, irregular

Ii

inhabit	v	live/reside/dwell/abide in, occupy
injure	v	hurt, harm, damage, wound, impair, spoil
inkling	n	hint, clue, suggestion, suspicion
innocent	adj	guiltless, blameless, harmless, simple
inquire (enquire)	v	ask, question, investigate
inquisitive	adj	curious, prying, inquiring (enquiring)
inside	adj adv	interior, internal, inner inward, inwards, within
insolent	adj	cheeky, impudent, rude, impertinent, insulting
inspect	v	check, examine, investigate
instant	n adj	moment, second, flash prompt, immediate, urgent
instruct	v	1 teach, train, coach, inform 2 order, command, direct, advise
insult	v	offend, cheek, abuse
intact	adj	complete, whole, sound, undamaged, unbroken, unharmed, untouched, entire
intelligent	adj	sensible, alert, astute, sharp, bright, clever, shrewd
intention	n	intent, aim, purpose, object, plan, design
intentional	adj	intended, deliberate, designed
interior	adj	inner, inside, internal
internal	adj	inner, inside, interior
interval	n	pause, gap, break, period
invade	v	enter uninvited, intrude, encroach
invent	v	discover, design, create, devise, imagine
investigate	v	inquire into, inspect, examine, check, search, study, probe
irksome	adj	tiresome, wearisome, boring, tedious

irritable	*adj*	fretful, peevish, easily annoyed, touchy
irritate	*v*	1 annoy, exasperate, provoke, anger, vex
		2 itch, chafe, make sore, inflame

Jj

jab	*v*	poke, stab, thrust, hit, punch
jagged	*adj*	coarse, notched, serrated, uneven
jail	*n*	prison, penitentiary, cell, dungeon
jam	*v*	squeeze, crush, crowd together, block, stop, cram, wedge
	n	conserve, preserve, confection
jar	*n*	pot, urn, vase, jug
	v	jolt, grate, scrape, shake, bump, jerk, push, knock, move, jostle
jaunt	*n*	outing, excursion, journey, ramble
jealous	*adj*	envious, grudging, resentful
jeer	*v*	sneer, taunt, scoff, make fun of, mock, gibe, laugh at, chaff, ridicule
jerk	*v*	yank, pull, push, tug, thrust, nudge, snatch, jump, jolt, jog, tremble, move, shake
jest	*v*	joke, banter, quip, gag, taunt
jewel	*n*	precious stone, gem
jig	*v*	dance, jump, skip, jog, trot, shake, jerk
jittery	*adj*	nervous, afraid, frightened, scared, timid, jumpy, anxious
job	*n*	1 task, work 2 business, occupation, trade, profession, employment, work
jog	*v*	1 shake, push, jerk, jolt, nudge 2 jig, dance, trot
join	*v*	fasten, tie, connect, bind, knot, attach, link, enter, merge, combine, unite
joke	*v*	jest, gag, quip, banter
jolly	*adj*	cheerful, happy, gay, joyful, joyous, merry, jovial, lively, pleasant, amusing, cheery
jolt	*n*	jerk, bump, blow, knock, jog, nudge, shock
	v	jerk, bump, knock, jog

jot	n	trifle, dot, fragment, iota
	v	write, note, record
journey	n	trip, voyage, excursion, expedition
joy	n	happiness, delight, joyfulness, glee, pleasure, merriment, gladness, jollity, bliss
judge	v	decide, estimate, consider, try, criticise, conclude
jumble	v	mix, muddle, disarrange, confuse, throw into disorder
	n	junk, oddments, rubbish
jump	v	leap, spring, skip, gambol, jig, jog, start, move, shake, jolt, jerk, bound
junk	n	jumble, oddments, waste, rubbish
just	adj	fair, right, true, honest, upright, righteous, straight, correct, proper, fitting, impartial
	adv	1 exactly, truly, quite, only, barely
		2 then, now, very recently
justice	n	fairness, right, fair treatment

Kk

keen   *adj*   1 sharp, cutting, piercing, bitter, strong, vivid, quick, alert, sensitive, acute
                                 2 willing, eager, zealous, enthusiastic, earnest, busy, active

keep   *v*   hold, save, possess, look after, preserve, guard, protect, reserve, retain, detain, remain, stay, observe

kidnap   *v*   abduct, carry off (a person), steal (a child)

kill   *v*   murder, slay, slaughter, put to death, massacre, destroy, execute, assassinate

kin   *n*   kindred, kinsfolk, family, relatives, relations

kind   *n*   sort, type, quality, character, nature, class
           adj   kind-hearted, thoughtful, considerate, friendly, gentle, tender, loving, affectionate, obliging

king   *n*   male ruler, monarch, sovereign

kingdom   *n*   realm, domain, dominion

kit   *n*   set, outfit, equipment, apparatus

knack   *n*   trick, method, cleverness, skill, art, habit

knave   *n*   rogue, rascal, scamp, scoundrel, villain

knock   *v*   strike, rap, hit, tap, punch, bump, bang
           n   blow, thud, tap

knot   *v*   tie, tangle, link, join, unite

know   *v*   1 understand, realize, comprehend
                                 2 recognize, identify

knowing   *adj*   well-informed, shrewd, cunning, artful, sharp, wide-awake, intelligent, clever, experienced

knowledge   *n*   learning, understanding, information, education

label	*n*	name, title, mark, stamp, seal
laborious	*adj*	tiring, fatiguing, wearisome, hard, difficult, heavy, painstaking, exhausting, tough, tiresome
labour	*n*	work, task, toil, effort, industry
lack	*v*	require, need, want
lag	*v*	linger, dawdle, loiter, straggle, delay
lame	*adj*	1 limping, crippled, injured 2 poor, unsatisfactory, feeble, unconvincing He gave us a **lame** excuse.
land	*n* *v*	1 earth, ground, soil 2 country, region, territory, district go ashore, beach, disembark
large	*adj*	big, great, grand, bulky, abundant, ample, plentiful, gigantic, massive, huge, immense
last	*adj* *v*	end, final, concluding hold out, stay, remain, persist, continue
lasting	*adj*	steady, constant, permanent
late	*adj*	1 behind time, overdue, delayed, slow 2 departed, dead, deceased
laugh	*v*	guffaw, chuckle, scoff, giggle, chortle
laughable	*adj*	amusing, funny, comic, comical, humorous, ridiculous
lax	*adj*	slack, easy, easygoing, careless, negligent, loose
layer	*n*	thickness, film, seam, coating
lazy	*adj*	idle, sluggish, slothful
lea	*n*	meadow, grassland
lead	*v*	1 guide, conduct, control, direct, steer, escort 2 excel, surpass, outstrip
leader	*n*	guide, chief, captain, commander, director

Ll

lean	v	incline, slant, slope, bend, rest
	adj	thin, lanky, slender, skinny
leap	v	jump, spring, bound, vault
learned	adj	wise, scholarly, well-educated
learning	n	knowledge, education
leave	v	depart, quit, go away, vacate, desert, forsake, abandon
	n	1 permission, consent 2 holiday, vacation
legend	n	story, tale, myth, fable
leisure	n	free time, ease, comfort, relaxation, rest
lengthen	v	make longer, stretch, extend, increase, prolong
lenient	adj	mild, gentle, easygoing, merciful, tolerant
let	v	allow, permit, consent to
level	adj	flat, even, smooth, straight
liberty	n	freedom, independence
lie	v	1 rest, recline 2 tell an untruth, fib
lift	v	raise, hoist, ascend, elevate
light	v	set on fire, ignite, illuminate, kindle
	adj	gentle, flimsy, frail, fragile
lighten	v	1 light up, brighten, illuminate 2 lessen, make less heavy, ease, relieve, reduce
like	v	love, approve of
	adj	alike, similar
limit	n	1 border, boundary, edge, frontier, end 2 restriction, check
limp	adj	slack, flabby, drooping, loose
	v	walk awkwardly/lamely
linger	v	delay, persist, dawdle, loiter, dally, lag

link	*v*	connect, join, attach, fasten, fix, unite, clasp
list	*n*	roll, register, catalogue, table, inventory
listless	*adj*	weary, tired, fatigued, feeble, drooping
litter	*n*	rubbish, refuse, waste, jumble
little	*adj* *n* *adv*	small, tiny, slight, miniature, minute small quantity, bit, scrap, morsel, fragment not much, slightly
live	*v* *adj*	exist, dwell, reside, stay, remain, abide living, alive, lively, active
lively	*adj*	1 active, brisk, nimble, alive, spritely, agile 2 cheerful, gay, jolly, merry, joyful, happy, bright, exciting
load	*n* *v*	burden, weight fill, charge
lofty	*adj*	1 high, towering, soaring, tall 2 proud, conceited, aloof, arrogant
loiter	*v*	hang about, dawdle, delay, linger
lonely	*adj*	lone, alone, solitary, forlorn, desolate
long	*adj* *v*	lengthy, far-reaching, endless desire, crave, yearn
look	*v*	1 observe, behold, watch, examine, inspect, contemplate, peep, glance, view, stare, gaze 2 search, seek 3 seem, appear
loose	*adj*	slack, detached, relaxed
lose	*v*	miss, mislay, drop
lot	*n*	1 much, many, all 2 items, articles 3 luck, fortune, fate, chance
loud	*adj*	1 noisy, deafening, blaring, booming, shrill 2 gaudy, bright, glaring, vivid, flashy

Ll

love	v	like, cherish, adore
	n	fondness, affection
lovely	*adj*	beautiful, attractive, pretty, charming, pleasing, delightful, enjoyable
loyal	*adj*	faithful, true, devoted, constant
luck	*n*	fate, fortune, lot, destiny, chance
lucky	*adj*	fortunate, favoured, successful, blessed
lull	*v*	soothe, quieten, calm
	n	pause, rest
lurk	*v*	hide, lie in wait, prowl, skulk, sneak
luxury	*n*	pleasure, enjoyment, delight

mad	*adj*	1 insane, deranged, crazy 2 angry, annoyed, furious, irate
magic	*n*	1 witchcraft, sorcery 2 conjuring, sleight-of-hand
magnificent	*adj*	grand, superb, splendid, beautiful, marvellous, majestic
magnify	*v*	make larger, enlarge, increase, exaggerate
maid	*n*	maiden, girl, miss, lass, damsel, wench
maim	*v*	injure, wound, hurt, cripple, mutilate, disable
main	*adj*	chief, central, most important, leading, principal
major	*adj*	great, large, significant, important
majority	*n*	greater part, most
make	*v*	1 do, perform, create, manufacture, construct, shape 2 force, compel, require
make-believe	*adj*	false, sham, pretended
malady	*n*	illness, sickness, ailment, disease
mammoth	*adj*	huge, gigantic, vast, immense, enormous
man	*n*	1 male, gentleman 2 workman, hand 3 mankind, the human race
manage	*v*	1 control, direct, run, organize, conduct, supervise 2 make do, get by, succeed
manageable	*adj*	orderly, disciplined, tame, obedient
manly	*adj*	strong, brave, noble, courageous, heroic
manner	*n*	1 way, method, kind, sort 2 style, fashion, behaviour
manners	*n*	conduct, behaviour, courtesy, politeness
manufacture	*v*	make, build, produce

Mm

many	*adj*	numerous, plenty, various
margin	*n*	edge, border, boundary, brim, verge, limit
mariner	*n*	sailor, seaman, seafarer
mark	*n*	1 token, sign, label, stamp, tag, seal 2 stain, scar, blemish, smudge
	v	1 observe, notice, note 2 point at, label, indicate
market	*n*	store, shops, shopping centre, bazaar
marsh	*n*	swamp, bog, morass, mire, fen, quagmire
marvellous	*adj*	wonderful, amazing, splendid, astonishing, extraordinary
mask	*v*	hide, conceal, disguise
mass	*n*	1 quantity, amount, weight, bulk 2 crowd, crush, mob
massive	*adj*	vast, immense, gigantic, huge, enormous
master	*n*	1 employer, director, chief, manager 2 expert, teacher, tutor, instructor
	v	overcome, conquer, tame, defeat, subdue
mate	*n*	1 husband, wife, partner 2 friend, chum, pal, companion, comrade
material	*n*	1 substance, matter 2 cloth, fabric
matter	*n*	1 substance, material 2 affair, business, event
	v	count, be important
maybe	*adv*	perhaps, possibly
meagre	*adj*	poor, small, slight, scanty, limited
mean	*adj*	1 poor, small, miserly, stingy 2 base, nasty, spiteful, unkind
	v	1 intend, aim, plan 2 show, indicate, signify
meaning	*n*	sense, explanation, purpose, definition

meaningless	*adj*	senseless, pointless, useless, idiotic
measure	*v*	find the size of, gauge, estimate, assess
mechanical	*adj*	automatic, machine-like, robotic
meddle	*v*	pry, tamper, interfere
meek	*adj*	mild, timid, gentle, humble, lowly, modest, docile, yielding
meet	*v*	1 encounter, confront 2 join, gather, assemble, unite, congregate
menace	*n*	threat, danger, peril
mend	*v*	repair, restore, fix, overhaul
mention	*v*	name, speak about, tell, report, disclose
merchant	*n*	trader, dealer, tradesman
mercy	*n*	pity, leniency, kindness, forgiveness, compassion, gentleness
merge	*v*	come together, join, mingle, combine
merit	*v*	deserve, earn, win
merry	*adj*	happy, gay, carefree, jolly, joyful, cheerful, jovial
mess	*n*	1 disorder, confusion, muddle 2 litter, rubbish, dirt
method	*n*	way, manner, system, procedure, process, course
middle	*adj*	central, midway, intermediate, half-way
might	*n*	force, power, strength, greatness
mild	*adj*	meek, timid, gentle, calm, placid, tender
mind	*n* *v*	brain, intellect, understanding, reason 1 look after, guard, watch, keep 2 obey, heed, listen to, observe 3 object to

Mm

miniature	*adj*	small, little, tiny
minor	*adj*	smaller, lesser, less important, lower
minority	*n*	smaller part, least
miraculous	*adj*	amazing, surprising, magical, astounding, astonishing
mirth	*n*	fun, laughter, glee, gaiety, merriment, amusement
mischief	*n*	1 naughtiness, pranks 2 damage, injury, harm
miserable	*adj*	sad, unhappy, gloomy, sorrowful, dejected, wretched, distressed, depressed
misfortune	*n*	bad luck, ill fortune, difficulty, calamity, disaster, mishap
miss	*v* *n*	1 overlook, leave out, avoid, omit 2 regret the absence of girl, young lady, unmarried woman, lass, maiden, damsel
mist	*n*	fog, cloud, haze, moisture, dew, vapour
mistake	*n*	error, fault, defect, misunderstanding, blunder
mix	*v*	blend, mingle, combine, unite
moan	*v*	groan, whimper, grumble, complain, lament
mob	*n*	crowd, rabble, mass
mock	*adj* *v*	sham, false, fake, imitation, tease jeer, imitate, ridicule, mimic
model	*n* *v*	example, specimen, pattern, design mould, shape, form, copy, design
modern	*adj*	new, up-to-date, current, recent
modest	*adj*	meek, humble, shy, retiring, bashful, unassuming
moist	*adj*	damp, wet, humid
moment	*n*	instant, second, flash

monarch	*n*	ruler, sovereign, king, queen, emperor, empress, chief
monotonous	*adj*	unchanging, dull, boring, wearisome, tedious, uniform
monster	*n*	cruel beast, huge animal, fiend, wicked person
moody	*adj*	sullen, sulky, peevish, gloomy
moreover	*adv*	furthermore, what is more, besides, also
morsel	*n*	bit, shred, scrap, fragment
motion	*n*	movement, action, gesture
motionless	*adj*	still, stationary, not moving
mount	*v*	1 climb, go up, rise, ascend, get on 2 place, set, display
mourn	*v*	grieve, lament
move	*v*	1 carry, transport, convey 2 travel, stir, shift 3 touch, excite, arouse, affect, impress
	n	step, action, decision
multiply	*v*	increase, make more
murder	*v*	kill, slaughter, slay, assassinate
must	*v*	should, ought to, have to
musty	*adj*	stale, mouldy, sour, foul
mutiny	*v*	disobey, rebel, revolt, rise
	n	rebellion, revolt, uprising, riot
mutter	*v*	murmur, mumble, grumble
mystery	*n*	puzzle, riddle, secret
myth	*n*	story, tale, fable, legend

Nn

nag	*v*	scold, chide, reprove, pester
naked	*adj*	nude, bare, unclothed, exposed, uncovered
name	*n*	title, label, term
narrow	*adj*	thin, slender, slim
nasty	*adj*	1 unpleasant, mean, spiteful 2 unclean, polluted, filthy
natural	*adj*	simple, like nature, normal, lifelike, usual
nature	*n*	1 creation, the universe 2 quality, manner, kind, sort, character
naughty	*adj*	mischievous, disobedient
near	*adv* *adj*	close, adjoining neighbouring, adjacent
nearly	*adv*	almost, all but, closely
neat	*adj*	tidy, clean, orderly, smart, trim, skilful
necessary	*adj*	needed, wanted, required, essential
need	*v* *n*	want, require, lack poverty, hardship, distress, necessity
needy	*adj*	in want, poor, destitute
neglect	*n* *v*	lack of care, carelessness, failure not care for, miss, fail, forget, disregard, omit
neglectful	*adj*	careless, forgetful, negligent, thoughtless
nerve	*n*	1 courage, pluck, daring, boldness 2 cheek, audacity, impudence
nervous	*adj*	fearful, afraid, timid, uneasy, shaky, jittery
new	*adj*	1 different, novel, original 2 recent, latest, fresh, unused, modern
news	*n*	reports, tidings, messages, information, bulletin

next	*adj*	nearest, following, after, adjacent
nice	*adj*	pleasant, good, agreeable, fine, delicious, attractive
nil	*n*	nothing, nought, zero
nimble	*adj*	quick, agile, lively, sprightly, skilful, active, alert
nip	*v*	bite, pinch, squeeze
noble	*adj*	worthy, great, splendid, honourable, lordly, majestic, gallant, dashing
nobleman	*n*	lord, peer, aristocrat, noble
noise	*n*	din, row, sound, clamour, tumult
nonsense	*n*	silliness, folly, rubbish, drivel, absurdity
normal	*adj*	usual, ordinary, general, natural, typical, regular
notice	*v* *n*	observe, see, note, heed 1 warning, advice 2 poster, circular, advertisement
notify	*v*	tell, inform, advise
nought	*n*	nothing, nil, zero
novel	*adj* *n*	new, original, fresh, strange, unusual story, tale, fiction, romance
nudge	*v*	tap, push, poke, prod
nuisance	*n*	pest, annoyance, bother, bore
number	*n* *v*	1 quantity, amount, sum, total 2 figure, digit, numeral count, reckon, total, compute
numerous	*adj*	many, a lot of, various, abundant

Oo

oaf	*n*	fool, idiot, lout
oath	*n*	1 solemn promise, pledge, vow 2 swear-word, blasphemy, curse
obedient	*adj*	dutiful, law-abiding, yielding, submissive
obey	*v*	observe, follow, submit to
object	*n*	1 thing, article, item 2 aim, intention, purpose, target, goal
	v	disapprove, protest, oppose
oblige	*v*	1 help, assist, aid 2 make, compel, expect, force
obscure	*adj*	1 dim, cloudy, hazy, unclear 2 unknown, doubtful, hidden, vague
observe	*v*	1 look at, see, watch, examine 2 remark, comment, mention 3 obey, submit to, follow
obstacle	*n*	hindrance, obstruction, bar, barrier, difficulty
obstinate	*adj*	stubborn, persistent, determined, inflexible, wilful
obstruct	*v*	hamper, block, impede, prevent
obtain	*v*	get, take, acquire, secure, gain
obvious	*adj*	clear, plain, apparent, unmistakable
occasion	*n*	happening, event, situation
occupation	*n*	work, job, trade, craft, profession, business, career, employment
occupy	*v*	live in, dwell in, reside in, inhabit
occur	*v*	happen, take place, befall
odd	*adj*	1 strange, peculiar, queer, unusual, extraordinary 2 uneven, not even, irregular
odour	*n*	smell, scent, aroma, fragrance, perfume
offend	*v*	displease, insult, vex, annoy, irritate

oO

offer	*v*	give, hold out, suggest
old	*adj*	aged, ancient, elderly, antique
omit	*v*	leave out, overlook, fail, exclude
only	*adj* *adv* *conj*	alone, lone, one, single singly, merely, nothing more than but then
open	*adj* *v*	1 not shut, uncovered, unclosed 2 sincere, frank, candid, honest 1 uncover, unfasten 2 begin, start, commence
opening	*n*	1 gap, break, hole, space, aperture 2 chance, opportunity, beginning, vacancy
operate	*v*	work, act, behave, manage
opinion	*n*	belief, comment, suggestion, view, judgement
opponent	*n*	rival, competitor, adversary, enemy, foe
opportunity	*n*	chance, opening
oppose	*v*	resist, obstruct, withstand
opposite	*adj*	contrary, facing, opposed
oppress	*v*	treat harshly, crush, burden
oral	*adj*	spoken, voiced, verbal, vocal
order	*n*	1 request, demand, rule, command, instruction 2 neatness, tidiness, method 3 arrangement, grade, class, rank
orderly	*adj*	1 ordered, neat, tidy, methodical, regular 2 disciplined, obedient, well-behaved
ordinary	*adj*	common, plain, normal, usual
organize	*v*	arrange, sort, plan
origin	*n*	source, start, cause, beginning
outing	*n*	trip, excursion, tour

Oo

outlaw	*n*	robber, bandit, brigand, highwayman
outside	*adv*	outward, outwards, without
	adj	external, exterior
over	*prep*	1 above, across
		2 more than
	adv	on the other side of
	adj	1 ended, finished, done with
		2 above, upper
overlook	*v*	ignore, excuse, pardon, forgive
overthrow	*v*	defeat, bring down, destroy
own	*v*	1 hold, have, possess
		2 confess, admit, grant, acknowledge

pace	*n*	1 stride, step, march, tread 2 speed, rate
pack	*n*	1 set, stack, collection 2 package, parcel, bundle, haversack, packet
	v	crowd together, cram, fill, compress
pain	*n*	ache, soreness, pang, twinge, agony, distress, suffering
pair	*n*	set of two, couple, brace
pc!	*n*	friend, chum, mate, companion, comrade
pale	*adj*	white, wan, ashen, grey, faint, dim, pallid
pamper	*v*	spoil, pet, coddle, indulge
panic	*n*	alarm, excitement, chaos, haste, frenzy, terror
parade	*n*	march, procession, display, pageant
parched	*adj*	1 dry, scorched, shrivelled, arid 2 thirsty
pardon	*v*	forgive, excuse, overlook
part	*n*	1 portion, fraction, bit, share, piece 2 character, role
	v	1 divide, separate, split, break 2 take, leave, quit
party	*n*	1 group, troop, band 2 feast, celebration
pass	*v*	1 go beyond, exceed 2 deliver, hand over 3 allow, permit, approve
	n	1 path, gap, opening 2 ticket, voucher, permit, passport
passage	*n*	1 corridor, route, way, alley 2 voyage, journey 3 part, section (of a book), sentence, paragraph
pastime	*n*	recreation, game, sport, amusement, hobby

Pp

patch	*v* *n*	cover, mend, repair 1 pad, strip, piece 2 plot, allotment
path	*n*	footpath, track, way, route, pavement
pattern	*n*	1 example, model, specimen, sample 2 design, decoration, figure, shape
pause	*n*	rest, interval, gap
peaceful	*adj*	quiet, calm, restful, serene
peak	*n*	top, tip, crown, summit, crest
peculiar	*adj*	strange, odd, queer, curious, unusual, rare
peer	*v* *n*	look, stare, peep, pry 1 equal, match 2 nobleman, aristocrat, lord
penetrate	*v*	enter, pass through, pierce, bore
people	*n*	persons, folk, individuals
perfect	*adj* *v*	excellent, faultless, ideal, superb, complete, exact, finished complete, improve, finish
perform	*v*	do, act, achieve, accomplish
perfume	*n*	scent, fragrance, aroma
perhaps	*adv*	maybe, possibly
peril	*n*	danger, risk, hazard
perish	*v*	1 die, expire 2 decay, rot, wither, shrivel
permanent	*adj*	lasting, constant, abiding, unchanging
permit	*v* *n*	allow, let, tolerate pass, licence, warrant
perplex	*v*	confuse, baffle, bewilder, puzzle
persecute	*v*	torment, ill-treat, oppress, molest
persevere	*v*	try, persist, strive
persist	*v*	persevere, strive, try, continue

persuade	*v*	urge, coax, encourage, influence
pest	*n*	nuisance, annoyance, plague, harmful animal
pet	*n*	1 favourite, darling 2 tame animal
	v	caress, fondle, cuddle
pick	*v*	1 choose, select, prefer 2 collect, gather, pluck, acquire
picture	*n*	illustration, sketch, drawing, photograph, painting, portrait, engraving
piece	*n*	part, portion, fraction, bit, fragment, morsel
pierce	*v*	penetrate, pass through, enter, stab, bore
pile	*n*	heap, stack, mound, collection
pilot	*n*	airman, navigator, helmsman
pinch	*v*	nip, squeeze, tweak
pine	*v*	1 yearn, long, crave 2 fret, waste away
pipe	*n*	tube, drain, conduit
pit	*n*	1 hole, hollow, cavity 2 mine, colliery
pitch	*v*	1 hurl, fling, throw, toss, cast 2 jolt, jump, shake
pity	*n*	sympathy, mercy, compassion, sorrow
place	*n*	spot, position, region, locality, situation
	v	put, set, lay, arrange, position, locate
plague	*v*	pester, tease, torment, annoy, bother, worry
plain	*adj*	1 simple, blunt, homely, undecorated 2 clear, obvious, distinct, apparent 3 level, even, smooth
plan	*n*	1 map, chart, diagram, drawing 2 scheme, idea, programme, proposal, project

Pp

plant	*v*	1 set, implant, sow 2 put, place, position
	n	herb, tree, shrub, weed
play	*v*	1 frolic, jest, frisk 2 act, perform
	n	drama, act, performance
plead	*v*	beg, implore, beseech
pleasant	*adj*	pleasing, agreeable, enjoyable, delightful
please	*v*	gladden, delight, satisfy, suit
pleasure	*n*	enjoyment, gladness, delight
plentiful	*adj*	abundant, ample, generous
plot	*n*	plan, scheme, design, project
pluck	*v*	gather, pick, snatch, pull
	n	bravery, courage, daring
plump	*adj*	fat, stout, chubby, rounded, bonny
plunder	*v*	loot, rob, steal, ravage
plunge	*v*	1 dive, dip, immerse, submerge 2 thrust, push, drive
point	*n*	1 tip, end 2 place, position, locality 3 purpose, object, aim
	v	aim, direct, level at
poke	*v*	prod, jab, nudge, push, thrust
polish	*v*	shine, buff, burnish, brighten
polite	*adj*	courteous, well-mannered, civil, cultured
poor	*adj*	1 needy, in want, impoverished 2 inferior, below standard, deficient
popular	*adj*	favourite, well-liked, admired, approved
population	*n*	people, inhabitants, citizens
portion	*n*	part, fraction, piece, bit, share, helping
position	*n*	place, spot, point, location, situation
	v	place, locate

possess	*v*	own, have, hold, control
possibly	*adv*	maybe, perhaps
poster	*n*	notice, placard, advertisement
postpone	*v*	put off, defer, delay, adjourn
pot	*n*	jar, vessel, dish, bowl
poverty	*n*	need, want, shortage, scarcity
power	*n*	1 control, mastery, authority, influence 2 strength, might, force, energy, ability
praise	*v*	commend, applaud, compliment, approve
precious	*adj*	valuable, prized, treasured, much-loved, cherished, adored
prefer	*v*	desire more, choose, fancy, select, pick
prepare	*v*	arrange, plan, make ready
present	*adj* *n* *v*	here, in person gift, offer, award, donation, gratuity 1 give, offer, bestow, donate, grant 2 introduce, announce, display **at present** now, this moment
presently	*adv*	shortly, soon, directly
preserve	*n* *v*	jam, jelly, pickles protect, guard, keep, defend, save
press	*v*	1 push, squeeze, crush, flatten 2 urge, compel, persuade, force
pressing	*adj*	urgent, immediate, important
pressure	*n*	force, effort, power
pretty	*adj*	attractive, lovely, beautiful, pleasing
prevent	*v*	avoid, check, stop, hinder, obstruct
previous	*adj*	earlier, recent, former, preceding
price	*n*	cost, charge, value

Pp

principle	*n*	rule, law, belief
prison	*n*	gaol, jail, penitentiary, cell, dungeon
private	*adj*	1 personal, individual, secret 2 remote, isolated, secluded
prize	*n*	reward, gift, honour, treasure, award, trophy
probable	*adv*	likely, possible, almost sure
problem	*n*	1 puzzle, riddle, exercise 2 difficulty, worry, trouble
proceed	*v*	1 begin, start, commence 2 travel, continue, resume
proclaim	*v*	tell, announce, declare, publish
produce	*v*	1 create, make, manufacture 2 give, yield
product	*n*	1 goods, item, article 2 result, consequence
profit	*n*	gain, benefit, advantage
programme	*n*	plan, scheme, schedule
progress	*v*	1 travel, advance, continue 2 improve, develop
project	*n*	plan, scheme, job, venture, proposal
promise	*v* *n*	intend, pledge, vow, assure vow, agreement, intention
promising	*adj*	hopeful, encouraging, optimistic
prompt	*adj* *v*	immediate, punctual, without delay, quick, fast, swift, rapid, speedy help, encourage, assist
proper	*adj*	correct, right, suitable, fitting
prosper	*v*	succeed, thrive, flourish, become wealthy
protect	*v*	defend, guard, shield, screen, shelter, preserve
protest	*v*	object, oppose, complain

proud	*adj*	1 vain, conceited, haughty 2 noble, dignified, splendid
provide	*v*	give, supply, prepare, produce
prowl	*v*	steal about, lurk, roam, wander
prudent	*adj*	wise, cautious, careful, discreet, wary
pull	*v*	drag, draw, tow, haul, yank, snatch, pluck, tear
punch	*v*	strike, thump, hit
punish	*v*	correct, discipline, chastise
puny	*adj*	weak, feeble, small, undersized
purchase	*v*	buy, acquire
pure	*adj*	1 clean, spotless, genuine, unmixed 2 innocent, blameless, virtuous, perfect, honest
purify	*v*	make pure, clean, cleanse
purpose	*n*	object, aim, intention, plan, design
pursue	*v*	hunt, chase, follow, seek
push	*v*	thrust, shove, press, jostle
puzzle	*n* *v*	problem, riddle baffle, mystify, confuse, bewilder, perplex

Qq

quaint	*adj*	odd, curious, unusual, unique
quake	*v*	shake, shiver, tremble, quiver, shudder, vibrate
qualified	*adj*	trained, fitted, capable, suitable
quality	*n*	kind, grade, standard, class, character
qualm	*n*	doubt, uneasiness, conscience, misgiving
quantity	*n*	amount, number, weight, size, volume, sum, portion, proportion, measure
quarrel	*n*	squabble, row, dispute, feud
quarry	*n*	hunted animal, prey, game
quarters	*n*	residence, home, abode
quash	*v*	crush, quell, cancel, ban, subdue, suppress
queen	*n*	female ruler/monarch/sovereign
queer	*adj*	odd, strange, unusual, peculiar, suspicious, doubtful, curious
quell	*v*	put down, overcome, crush, subdue, suppress, overpower
quench	*v*	1 extinguish, put out (fire) 2 slake (thirst), satisfy
quest	*n*	search, inquiry, hunt
question	*v*	inquire (enquire), ask, examine, dispute
questionable	*adj*	doubtful, uncertain, unsure, unreliable, suspicious
quick	*adj*	1 rapid, fast, speedy, swift, fleet, brisk, agile, nimble, spry, energetic, active, lively, alert, keen, eager 2 sudden, immediate 3 sharp, short, snappy, abrupt, hasty, impatient, harsh
quiet	*adj*	1 silent, noiseless, hushed 2 still, restful, peaceful, tranquil, calm

quieten	*v*	calm, soothe, pacify
quit	*v*	1 leave, depart from, vacate 2 forsake, abandon, give up, resign, renounce 3 stop, cease, discontinue
quite	*adv*	1 completely, entirely, wholly, totally, truly, really 2 rather, fairly, more or less
quiver	*v*	tremble, shake, shiver, shudder, quake, twitch

Rr

race	v	sprint, dash, run, flow
	n	1 contest, competition
		2 tribe, people, clan, nation
racket	n	1 din, row, noise, uproar, commotion, tumult
		2 bat, racquet
		3 fraud, swindle
rage	n	anger, fury, wrath, passion
ragged	adj	torn, tattered, shabby
raid	v	attack, invade, plunder
rail	n	bar, beam, fence, barrier
raise	v	1 erect, lift, hoist
		2 increase, advance
		3 grow, rear, breed
		4 bring up, educate (children)
		5 collect, gather (taxes)
		6 stir up, rouse, excite
rank	n	1 line, row, queue
		2 class, quality, position, order
	adj	1 coarse, gross, choked
		2 rotting, decaying, foul
		3 glaring, undisguised
ransack	v	search, loot, plunder, pillage
rap	n	1 tap, knock, thump
		2 jot, bit
rapid	adj	quick, fast, swift, speedy
rare	adj	uncommon, unusual, scarce, exceptional
rascal	n	rogue, scamp, scoundrel, villain
rash	adj	reckless, wild, headstrong, hasty, careless
rate	n	1 price, cost, charge, value
		2 speed, pace, swiftness, velocity
rather	adv	1 sooner, for choice, preferably
		2 slightly, somewhat
rattle	n	noise, sound, din, clatter
rave	v	rage, rant, roar, howl
ravenous	adj	very hungry, starving, famished

raw	*adj*	1 fresh, uncooked, unprepared 2 sore, sensitive, bare 3 cold, chilly, bitter, damp, bleak
ready	*adj*	1 willing, available, handy, prepared 2 prompt, immediate, quick
real	*adj*	true, genuine, actual, natural
realize	*v*	understand, know, are aware, appreciate
really	*adv*	indeed, truly, certainly, positively
rear	*adj* *n* *v*	back, hindmost, rearmost end, back, background 1 bring up, train, educate (children) 2 raise, breed 3 build, erect, construct
reason	*n*	1 cause, purpose, aim, motive 2 mind, intellect
reasonable	*adj*	fair, just, proper, sensible, honest
rebel	*v*	disobey, revolt, mutiny, resist
recall	*v*	1 remember, recollect 2 call back, bring back
receive	*v*	accept, gain, obtain, acquire
recent	*adj*	latest, new, modern
recite	*v*	repeat, relate, retell, recount
reckless	*adj*	rash, thoughtless, wild, careless, hasty
recognize	*v*	1 remember, know, identify 2 accept, acknowledge, admit
recollect	*v*	recall, remember, call to mind
recover	*v*	1 get back, regain, restore, retrieve 2 get better, improve, revive
recreation	*n*	leisure, pastime, amusement, game, sport, hobby
reduce	*v*	lessen, decrease, shrink, contract, shorten
refuge	*n*	shelter, retreat, haven, sanctuary, harbour

Rr

regain	v	get back, recover, retrieve
regard	v	look at, view, behold, observe, notice
region	n	area, district, land, territory
regret	v	grieve, lament, deplore
regular	adj	usual, proper, constant, normal
relate	v	tell, say, describe, recount, report
relax	v	1 take ease, rest 2 reduce, loosen, slacken
release	v	free, let go, unfasten
reliable	adj	dependable, trustworthy, loyal, accurate
rely	v	depend, trust, count
remain	v	1 stay, rest, tarry 2 last, survive
remark	v	say, comment, mention, state
remarkable	adj	unusual, uncommon, noteworthy, exceptional, strange, striking
remedy	n	cure, medicine, treatment
remember	v	recall, recollect, bring to mind
remote	adj	distant, far away, lonely, isolated, secluded
remove	v	1 take away, displace, detach 2 carry, convey, transfer
repair	v	remedy, restore, mend, renovate, patch
repay	v	pay back, reward, return, restore
repeat	v	do again, retell, recite, quote
replace	v	1 put back, return, restore 2 succeed, substitute
reply	n, v	answer, retort, echo
report	n	1 message, news, rumour, account, statement 2 explosion, bang, noise

request	*v*	ask for, demand, require
require	*v*	want, need, desire, demand
rescue	*v*	remove from danger, save, recover, release
reserve	*v*	store, save, set aside, retain
reserved	*adj*	1 booked, saved, kept, retained 2 shy, modest, retiring
reside	*v*	live, dwell, abide, occupy, inhabit
resist	*v*	withstand, oppose, defy
respect	*n*	esteem, admiration, regard
respond	*v*	reply, answer
restful	*adj*	quiet, relaxing, leisurely, peaceful
restless	*adj*	uneasy, fidgety, impatient, restive
restore	*v*	replace, return, repay, refund
restrict	*v*	control, hold back, limit, restrain, confine
result	*n*	outcome, effect, answer, conclusion
resume	*v*	start again, recommence, go on, continue, renew
retain	*v*	keep, hold
retire	*v*	go back, withdraw, retreat
retort	*n*	reply, response, answer
return	*v*	1 put back, restore, replace 2 reappear, come back
reveal	*v*	show, unmask, disclose, divulge, uncover
reverse	*v*	1 turn round, invert 2 travel backwards
	n	1 opposite side, inverted 2 defeat, failure, loss
reward	*n*	prize, payment, gift, bounty

Rr

rich   *adj*   1 wealthy, prosperous
                                  2 abundant, thick, fertile
                                  3 bright, deep, vivid

riddle   *n*   problem, puzzle, mystery, conundrum

ridicule   *v*   mock, tease, taunt
                 n   scorn, mockery, jeers

ridiculous   *adj*   silly, absurd, foolish, unreasonable

right   *adj*   correct, proper, fair, just, exact, true

rigid   *adj*   1 stiff, firm, unbending
                                  2 harsh, strict, inflexible, stern

ring   *n*   circle, band, loop
                 v   1 chime
                                    2 telephone

ripe   *adj*   full-grown, ready, mellow, mature

rise   *v*   1 arise, stand up
                                  2 ascend, climb, mount
                                  3 increase, swell, enlarge
                 n   hill, mound, slope

risk   *n*   chance, danger, hazard, peril

road   *n*   highway, route, way

roam   *v*   wander, ramble, stray, stroll

rob   *v*   steal, plunder, pilfer, pillage

robber   *n*   bandit, thief, pirate, highwayman

rock   *v*   sway, swing, stagger
                 n   stone, pebble, boulder

rogue   *n*   rascal, scamp, scoundrel, villain, cheat

roll   *v*   1 rotate, revolve, wind, spin
                                  2 flatten, level, press, smooth

rot   *v*   decay, perish, spoil

rough   *adj*   1 coarse, jagged, uneven
                                  2 wild, stormy, disorderly
                                  3 severe, harsh
                                  4 vulgar, rude, uncouth

rouse   *v*   wake, stir up, alarm, awaken, provoke

rout	*v*	defeat, beat, vanquish, conquer
route	*n*	way, road, course, path
row	*n*	1 quarrel, disagreement, dispute 2 noise, din, uproar, commotion
rub	*v*	1 stroke, massage 2 smear, wipe
rubbish	*n*	waste, junk, refuse, litter, debris
rude	*adj*	vulgar, coarse, impolite, insolent, ignorant
ruin	*v*	wreck, destroy, spoil
rumour	*n*	gossip, hearsay, talk, report
run	*v*	1 race, sprint, dash, flow 2 manage, direct, control
rush	*v*	move quickly, hasten, hurry, stampede

Ss

sacred	*adj*	holy, religious, hallowed, consecrated
sad	*adj*	unhappy, sorrowful, miserable, gloomy, dejected, forlorn, melancholy, depressed
safe	*adj*	1 secure, protected, guarded 2 trustworthy, reliable, sure
sample	*n*	example, specimen, pattern, model
satisfy	*v*	please, suit, content, gratify
saucy	*adj*	cheeky, rude, impudent, impertinent, insolent
savage	*adj*	1 wild, untamed, cruel, brutal, fierce 2 angry, enraged, furious, violent, brutal
save	*v*	1 rescue, help, assist 2 protect, store, keep, collect
say	*v*	tell, state, declare, speak, express
scarce	*adj*	rare, short, few, uncommon
scare	*v*	frighten, alarm, startle, terrify
scatter	*v*	1 spread, sprinkle, strew 2 separate, disperse
scent	*n*	smell, odour, perfume, aroma, fragrance
scheme	*n*	plan, design, plot, project
scoff	*v*	sneer, mock, ridicule
scold	*v*	nag, chide, reprove, reprimand, rebuke
scoundrel	*n*	rogue, rascal, villain, cheat
scrap	*n*	1 bit, shred, fragment 2 waste, rubbish, refuse 3 quarrel, fight, brawl
scratch	*v*	tear, claw, mark, score
scream	*v*	bawl, yell, shriek, screech
search	*v*	seek, explore, examine, investigate
secret	*adj*	hidden, concealed, mysterious

section	*n*	part, piece, division, segment
secure	*adj*	safe, fast, tight
	v	1 obtain, get, acquire
		2 fasten, tie up, lock
see	*v*	1 observe, watch, examine, perceive
		2 know, understand, grasp
seize	*v*	1 hold, grasp, grip, capture, arrest
		2 steal, rob, snatch, grab
seldom	*adv*	not often, rarely, occasionally
select	*v*	pick, choose, prefer
selfish	*adj*	greedy, mean, covetous, inconsiderate
send	*v*	dispatch (despatch), forward, drive
sensible	*adj*	intelligent, wise, alert, practical
separate	*adj*	apart, individual, detached, divided, distinct
	v	divide, detach, part
serene	*adj*	calm, tranquil, peaceful, placid, composed
series	*n*	sequence, list
serious	*adj*	1 grave, solemn, important
		2 thoughtful, sincere, responsible
set	*v*	1 place, put, stand, plant, arrange
		2 harden, solidify
	n	pack, kit, outfit
settle	*v*	1 rest, alight
		2 arrange, decide, agree
severe	*adj*	1 stern, strict, harsh, rigid
		2 plain, simple
		3 violent, serious
shabby	*adj*	1 ragged, worn, drab
		2 mean, spiteful, unfair
shady	*adj*	1 shaded, darkened, gloomy
		2 dishonest, crooked, suspicious
shake	*v*	1 tremble, shiver, shudder, vibrate, quake
		2 wave, brandish, flourish

Ss

shame	*n*	disgrace, dishonour, guilt
shape	*v*	form, fashion, mould
	n	form, figure, outline
share	*n*	part, portion, division
sharp	*adj*	1 keen, pointed, acute 2 painful, stinging, acid, harsh 3 alert, bright, intelligent, clever, smart
sheer	*adj*	1 abrupt, steep 2 complete, utter
shelter	*n*	shield, cover, protection, haven
shield	*n*	shelter, screen, cover, guard, protection
shine	*v*	glow, glisten, gleam, reflect, sparkle
	n	brightness, brilliance, gloss, polish
shiver	*v*	shake, tremble, quake, shudder, vibrate
shock	*v*	frighten, alarm, startle, dismay
short	*adj*	1 brief, concise 2 scanty, lacking 3 abrupt, sharp, hasty, curt
shout	*v*	call loudly, yell, scream, exclaim, bellow
show	*v*	1 indicate, display, reveal 2 explain, guide
shred	*n*	scrap, flake, fragment, piece
shrill	*adj*	keen, piercing, loud
shut	*adj*	closed, fastened
shy	*adj*	timid, modest, bashful, reserved
sick	*adj*	ill, unwell, ailing
sign	*n*	signal, mark, badge, symbol, emblem
silent	*adj*	quiet, noiseless, still
silly	*adj*	foolish, senseless, stupid
similar	*adj*	resembling, alike

simple	*adj*	1 easy, not difficult 2 plain, homely, neat 3 open, frank, honest, sincere
sincere	*adj*	honest, true, genuine
site	*n*	place, position, situation, spot
skilful	*adj*	skilled, expert, efficient
slack	*adj*	1 loose, limp, flabby, relaxed 2 lazy, idle, lax
slay	*v*	kill, murder, slaughter, massacre, assassinate
sleek	*adj*	smooth, glossy, silky
sleep	*v*	slumber, repose, doze, snooze
slender	*adj*	1 slim, thin, narrow 2 slight, scanty, meagre
slight	*adj* *v*	1 small, trifling, petty 2 slim, slender, delicate insult, ignore, snub
slim	*adj*	slender, thin, narrow
slip	*v* *n*	stumble, stagger, fall, slide mistake, error, fault
sly	*adj*	crafty, cunning, underhand
small	*adj*	little, tiny, slight, trivial
smart	*adj*	1 clever, intelligent, bright, expert 2 neat, tidy, stylish 3 sharp, biting, stinging, keen
smell	*n*	scent, odour, fragrance, aroma
smooth	*adj*	even, flat, plain, polished
snatch	*v*	grab, grip, seize, grasp, pluck
sob	*v*	cry, weep, gulp
soft	*adj*	1 weak, limp, pliable, 2 gentle, tender, mild, lenient
soggy	*adj*	wet, soaked, moist, damp
solemn	*adj*	serious, grave, dignified, important

Ss

solid	*adj*	firm, rigid, hard, compact
soothe	*v*	ease, calm, relieve
sore	*adj*	painful, tender, smarting, raw
sorrow	*n*	sadness, misery, grief, woe, distress, mourning
sorry	*adj*	1 sorrowful, grieved, regretful 2 poor, sad, wretched, miserable
sort	*n*	kind, type, group, species
sound	*n* *adj*	noise, din, clamour 1 wise, sensible, reliable 2 whole, complete, fit, healthy
sour	*adj*	acid, tart, bitter, sharp
source	*n*	origin, beginning
space	*n*	1 room, accommodation 2 break, gap
spare	*adj* *v*	scanty, poor, thin, sparse, lean let go, not harm, free, show mercy to
sparkle	*v*	flash, glisten, twinkle, gleam
speak	*v*	talk, say, tell, declare, proclaim, announce
speed	*n*	quickness, haste, swiftness, promptness, pace, velocity
spin	*v*	turn, whirl, twist, revolve, rotate
spite	*n*	malice, hatred, dislike
splendid	*adj*	grand, fine, magnificent, superb, delightful, excellent, glorious
spoil	*v*	ruin, destroy, damage, harm
sport	*n*	game, pastime, amusement, hobby, pursuit
spread	*v*	cover, scatter, sow, distribute, disperse
spring	*v*	leap, jump, bound, vault
squabble	*v*	quarrel, bicker, argue

squeeze	*v*	press, crush, squash, embrace
squirm	*v*	wriggle, writhe, twist
stab	*v*	pierce, puncture, enter
stain	*v*	mark, blot, smear, discolour, tarnish
stand	*v*	1 erect, be upright 2 abide, suffer, endure
	n	support, prop, rest
start	*v*	1 begin, commence, open 2 go, leave, depart
startle	*v*	frighten, alarm, surprise, shock
state	*v*	say, relate, voice, declare
	n	1 condition, quality 2 country, nation
stay	*v*	remain, rest, abide
steady	*adj*	firm, still, calm, stable
steal	*v*	rob, thieve, pilfer, plunder
stern	*adj*	strict, harsh, severe, hard
stiff	*adj*	rigid, firm, unbending
still	*adj*	calm, steady, quiet, motionless
stir	*v*	rouse, excite, agitate, provoke
stop	*v*	1 cease, end, finish 2 halt, check, arrest, prevent 3 stay, remain, pause
store	*n*	1 supply, stock, reserve 2 shop, warehouse, supermarket
storm	*n*	1 wind, gale, tempest, hurricane 2 rage, fury, temper
story	*n*	1 tale, yarn, account, record 2 lie, falsehood, untruth
stout	*adj*	1 fat, plump 2 firm, strong, sturdy 3 bold, brave, staunch, gallant

Ss

straight	*adj*	1 level, flat, even 2 tidy, clear, right 3 honest, genuine, direct, sincere, fair
strange	*adj*	queer, odd, peculiar, unused
strict	*adj*	severe, stern, harsh
strike	*v*	hit, knock, beat, slap, attack
strong	*adj*	1 powerful, vigorous, sturdy 2 glaring, brilliant, vivid, dazzling
stubborn	*adj*	obstinate, unbending, headstrong, inflexible
stumble	*v*	stagger, trip, fall
stupid	*adj*	foolish, silly, absurd, ridiculous, senseless
style	*n*	fashion, manner, way, method
succeed	*v*	prosper, achieve, flourish
sudden	*adj*	quick, abrupt, unexpected, rapid
suffer	*v*	1 undergo, stand, abide 2 permit, allow, tolerate
suitable	*adj*	proper, fitting, satisfactory
super	*adj*	wonderful, marvellous, superb, tremendous
superb	*adj*	splendid, grand, magnificent
supply	*v* *n*	provide, furnish store, stock, reserve
support	*v*	1 aid, assist, help, encourage, defend 2 hold up, prop
suppose	*v*	fancy, think, imagine, believe, assume
sure	*adj*	1 certain, confident, definite, convinced 2 safe, reliable, secure
surly	*adj*	sullen, sulky, moody, morose
surprise	*v*	astonish, amaze, shock, startle
surprised	*adj*	astonished, amazed, shocked, startled

suspicious	*adj*	doubtful, dubious, distrustful, jealous
sweet	*adj*	sugary, pleasing, fragrant
swell	*v*	enlarge, inflate, bulge, expand
swift	*adj*	quick, fast, rapid, speedy, hasty, hurried

Tt

tactful	*adj*	prudent, discreet, cautious
taint	*v*	spoil, soil, stain, infect, corrupt, pollute
take	*v*	1 remove, receive, grasp, seize 2 lead, conduct, carry, accompany
tale	*n*	story, yarn, account
talent	*n*	skill, ability, aptitude
talk	*v*	speak, discuss, gossip, converse
tall	*adj*	high, lofty, steep
tame	*adj*	timid, domesticated, docile
tasty	*adj*	delicious, savoury
teach	*v*	train, instruct, educate
tease	*v*	torment, annoy, taunt
tell	*v*	relate, reveal, mention, inform, describe
tempt	*v*	entice, attract, lure, persuade
tender	*adj*	1 soft, gentle, mild 2 kind, loving, affectionate 3 sore, painful
terrible	*adj*	dreadful, frightful, terrifying, awful, horrid
terrific	*adj*	1 huge, enormous, gigantic 2 wonderful, marvellous, superb
terrified	*adj*	in terror, frightened, alarmed, scared
terror	*n*	dread, horror, fright
test	*v*	try, examine, check, inspect
thankful	*adj*	grateful, obliged
theft	*n*	robbery, stealing, pilfering
thick	*adj*	1 deep, broad, wide 2 swarming, crowded, packed, plentiful
thin	*adj*	1 lean, slender, slim, narrow 2 scanty, sparse

think	v	imagine, fancy, believe, reason
thorough	adj	complete, entire, full, accurate
though	conj	although, if, even if
thought	n	belief, idea, opinion, view
thrash	v	beat, strike, belabour
threaten	v	warn, menace
throw	v	hurl, fling, heave, cast, toss
tidings	n	news, messages
tidy	adj	clean, neat, orderly, trim
tight	adj	stretched, secure, fast
timid	adj	shy, retiring, afraid
tiny	adj	very small, minute, little
tired	adj	weary, fatigued, exhausted
toil	v	work, labour, strive
top	n	highest point, summit, head, apex
torment	v	torture, tease, annoy, irritate
tough	adj	hard, strong, firm
trace	v	trail, find, discover
train	v	teach, instruct, educate, prepare
trap	n	1 snare, ambush 2 trick, deception
	v	catch, capture, snare, ambush
travel	v	move, journey, voyage
treat	v	handle, manage, deal with
tremble	v	shake, shiver, shudder, quiver
tremendous	adj	immense, huge, enormous, colossal
trick	v	1 puzzle, deceive, baffle 2 swindle, cheat, defraud, deceive, dupe

Tt

trip	*n*	journey, tour, outing, excursion
triumph	*n*	success, achievement, victory
trouble	*n*	1 bother, worry, plight 2 care, effort, pains
	v	disturb, pester, annoy
true	*adj*	1 real, genuine, actual, authentic 2 faithful, loyal, sincere, reliable
trust	*n*	belief, faith, confidence
trustworthy	*adj*	reliable, faithful, loyal, dependable
truth	*n*	honesty, accuracy, frankness
truthful	*adj*	honest, open, sincere, candid
try	*v*	attempt, endeavour
turn	*v*	1 change, alter, convert 2 roll, spin, twist, wind, revolve, rotate
twist	*v*	1 wind, turn, rotate 2 curve, bend, distort

ugly	*adj*	1 repulsive, hideous, unsightly 2 unpleasant, threatening, dangerous
unaware	*adj*	not aware, ignorant, heedless
uncertain	*adj*	unsure, undecided, doubtful, changeable
uncommon	*adj*	unusual, rare, strange
uncover	*v*	reveal, disclose, expose
undecided	*adj*	uncertain, unsure, doubtful, hesitating
under	*prep*	beneath, below, lower than
underhand	*adj*	deceitful, treacherous, sly, secret
understand	*v*	know, grasp, perceive
undisturbed	*adj*	untroubled, calm, confident, peaceful
unearth	*v*	discover, find, reveal
uneasy	*adj*	restless, worried, disturbed, uncomfortable, impatient
uneven	*adj*	rough, coarse, irregular
unexpected	*adj*	unforeseen, sudden, surprising, abrupt
unfair	*adj*	unjust, wrongful, improper, unequal
unfaithful	*adj*	disloyal, untrue, deceitful, treacherous
unfasten	*v*	undo, free, untie, disconnect, release
unfit	*adj*	unhealthy, unwell, ailing
unfortunate	*adj*	unlucky, ill-fated, unsuccessful
unfriendly	*adj*	hostile, unkind, cold
unhappy	*adj*	sad, miserable, sorrowful, depressed
unhealthy	*adj*	unfit, sickly, diseased
unimportant	*adj*	trivial, commonplace, ordinary, petty
unjust	*adj*	unfair, improper, wrongful
unkind	*adj*	harsh, unpleasant, spiteful, cruel
unknown	*adj*	undiscovered, unexplored, anonymous

Uu

unlikely	*adj*	improbable
unlucky	*adj*	unfortunate, ill-fated, unsuccessful
unpleasant	*adj*	displeasing, disagreeable, unwelcome, offensive
unruly	*adj*	rowdy, disorderly, disobedient
unsafe	*adj*	dangerous, hazardous, unguarded, perilous
untidy	*adj*	slovenly, disorderly
until	*prep*	till, up to, to the time of
untrue	*adj*	1 false, mistaken, incorrect, inaccurate 2 unfaithful, disloyal, false
unusual	*adj*	uncommon, strange, rare, remarkable, curious
unwise	*adj*	foolish, rash, unthinking
upright	*adj*	1 erect, vertical 2 honest, true, straight, trustworthy
uproar	*n*	chaos, panic, disturbance, tumult, noise
upset	*v*	1 overturn, topple, knock over, capsize 2 trouble, worry, annoy, confuse
urge	*v*	press, beg, beseech, persuade, implore
urgent	*adj*	pressing, important
use	*v*	1 employ, apply 2 consume, exhaust, waste
useful	*adj*	helpful, valuable, convenient
usual	*adj*	common, ordinary, normal, regular, general
utter	*v* *adj*	speak, say, declare, pronounce complete, total, entire

vacant	*adj*	1 empty, unoccupied, free 2 dreamy, stupid, thoughtless
vagabond	*n*	tramp, wanderer, vagrant, rascal, rogue
vague	*adj*	unclear, uncertain, doubtful, hazy, misty, dim
vain	*adj*	1 proud, conceited, pompous 2 useless, pointless, unsuccessful **in vain** without success, useless
valiant	*adj*	brave, fearless, heroic, daring, courageous, gallant, bold
valley	*n*	vale, dale, hollow, ravine
valuable	*adj*	worthwhile, useful
value	*n*	1 worth, merit, quality, importance 2 cost, price, rate
vanish	*v*	disappear, become invisible
variety	*n*	1 sort, kind, type, class, species 2 mixture, assortment, difference
various	*adj*	different, varied, miscellaneous
vary	*v*	differ, change, modify
vast	*adj*	huge, enormous, gigantic, immense
verbal	*adj*	oral, vocal, spoken
vertical	*adj*	upright, erect, perpendicular
vessel	*n*	1 container, receptacle, jar, pot, bottle, dish, can, bin, utensil 2 ship, boat
vex	*v*	anger, annoy, irritate, torment
vicious	*adj*	wicked, evil, violent
victory	*n*	triumph, success, win, conquest
view	*n*	1 scene, sight 2 opinion, purpose, belief
	v	see, observe, watch, examine

Vv

vigorous	*adj*	lively, energetic, brisk, forceful, strong, healthy
vile	*adj*	evil, wicked, unpleasant, repulsive
villain	*n*	criminal, rogue, rascal, scoundrel
violent	*adj*	forceful, powerful, rough, fierce, savage, wild, frantic
virtue	*n*	goodness, purity, excellence
vision	*n*	1 eyesight, sight 2 image, dream, ghost, phantom
visit	*v*	call upon, stay with
vital	*adj*	essential, very important, much needed
vivid	*adj*	very clear, glaring, bright, brilliant, intense
vocal	*adj*	spoken, oral, said, sung, verbal
voice	*v*	utter, say, declare
volume	*n*	capacity, size, bulk, content, mass
vow	*n*	promise, oath, pledge
voyage	*n*	sea journey, cruise
vulgar	*adj*	common, coarse, uncouth, rude, vile

wage	n	pay, payment, earnings
wait	v	stay, stop, rest, remain, linger
waken	v	awaken, wake, rouse, bestir
wander	v	stray, roam, ramble, stroll
wane	v	weaken, fall, sink, decrease
want	v	1 desire, crave, wish 2 lack, need, require
warn	v	caution, threaten, advise
wary	adj	alert, watchful, wise, cautious, careful, guarded
waste	v	1 squander, spoil, use extravagantly 2 wither, fade, decay, dwindle
	n	1 rubbish, refuse, junk 2 extravagance 3 desert, wilderness
wasteful	adj	extravagant, thriftless
watch	v	1 observe, look at, notice 2 guard, protect
waver	v	hesitate, falter, pause, fluctuate
way	n	1 path, road, route, direction, course 2 method, manner, fashion, plan
wayward	adj	contrary, awkward, difficult, obstinate
weak	adj	feeble, frail, delicate, fragile, sickly, helpless, infirm
wealth	n	riches, money, prosperity, assets, fortune
weary	adj	tired, fatigued, exhausted
weep	v	cry, shed tears, sob
weird	adj	strange, odd, uncanny
wet	adj	sodden, soaked, drenched, moist, saturated
whim	n	fancy, craze, idea, impulse
whirl	v	spin, turn, twist, revolve, rotate

Ww

white	*adj*	1 pale, ashen, snowy, pallid 2 spotless, clean
whole	*adj*	1 complete, entire, full 2 sound, healthy, well
wicked	*adj*	1 evil, vile, vicious, sinful, corrupt 2 mischievous, naughty, cheeky
wide	*adj*	broad, vast, spacious
wild	*adj*	untamed, savage, reckless, ferocious
wilderness	*n*	desert, waste, barren land
wilful	*adj*	1 deliberate, intentional 2 awkward, mischievous, stubborn
win	*v*	gain, earn, capture, achieve
wind	*n* *v*	breeze, gust, gale turn, reel, wander, coil
wise	*adj*	sensible, intelligent, prudent
wish	*v*	want, desire, hope, long
wit	*n*	1 sense, intelligence, wisdom, reason 2 witticism, humour
within	*adv*	inside, indoors, inwardly
without	*prep* *adv*	lacking, in want of outside, out-of-doors
withstand	*v*	resist, oppose
wonder	*v*	1 marvel 2 doubt, consider, question
wonderful	*adj*	marvellous, splendid, superb, amazing, astounding, extraordinary
work	*n*	1 labour, effort, toil, task 2 job, trade, business, profession, occupation, employment 3 achievement, feat, deed
worn	*adj*	1 used, threadbare, shabby 2 tired, weary, fatigued
worry	*v* *n*	bother, trouble, disturb, sadden, fret problem, care, anxiety, concern

worship	*v*	adore, idolize, honour, respect
worth	*n*	value, cost, price
worthless	*adj*	valueless, useless, pointless
worthy	*adj*	decent, worthwhile, honourable, honest, deserving
wound	*v*	injure, maim, hurt, damage, harm
wrath	*n*	anger, rage, fury, indignation
wreck	*v*	ruin, destroy, spoil, break, shatter
wreckage	*n*	remains, debris, flotsam
wretched	*adj*	1 miserable, pathetic, pitiful, unhappy 2 mean, unworthy, despised
writhe	*v*	twist, wriggle, squirm
wrong	*adj*	1 incorrect, inaccurate, unsuitable 2 wicked, improper, unfair
	n	injury, sin, injustice, unfairness
	v	injure, hurt, harm, abuse
Xmas	*n*	Christmas

yank	*v*	jerk, pull, snatch
yarn	*n*	story, tale
yearly	*adv* *adj*	annually, each year, every year annual
yearn	*v*	long, crave, pine, desire
yell	*v*	bawl, scream, screech, shout
yet	*adv*	1 still, at present, so far 2 also, again, further 3 however, nevertheless, but for all that
yield	*v* *n*	1 produce, give, supply, provide 2 submit, surrender, resign product, crop, harvest, output
young	*adj*	youthful, juvenile
youth	*n*	juvenile, teenage boy
zeal	*n*	enthusiasm, eagerness, keenness, energy
zero	*n*	nothing, nought, nil
zest	*n*	enthusiasm, eagerness, relish
zigzag	*adj*	jagged, twisted, crooked

Aa   Opposites   Bb

abandon	v	keep, occupy, adopt
able	adj	unable
above	adv	below, beneath, under
abroad	adv	near, here, at home
abrupt	adj	slow, gentle, courteous
absent	adj	present, here
absurd	adj	sound, sensible
abundant	adj	scarce, short
accept	v	refuse, reject, decline
accurate	adj	inaccurate, doubtful
accuse	v	excuse
achieve	v	fail, lose
active	adj	inactive
acute	adj	mild
add	v	subtract
adequate	adj	inadequate
adjacent	adj	distant, apart
admit	v	deny, forbid
adopt	v	forsake, abandon
adore	v	hate, detest
adult	n	child
advance	v	retreat
advantage	n	disadvantage
afraid	adj	unafraid
after	adv	before
age	n	youth
agile	adj	clumsy
agree	v	disagree
agreeable	adj	disagreeable
ahead	adv	behind
aid	v	hinder
alight	v	mount
alive	adj	dead
allow	v	disallow
always	adv	never
amateur	n	professional
amuse	v	bore
ancient	adj	modern
anger	v	please
annoy	v	soothe

answer	n	question
anxiety	n	contentment
appear	v	disappear
approve	v	disapprove
arouse	v	soothe
arrange	v	disarrange
arrest	v	release
arrive	v	depart
ascend	v	descend
ashamed	adj	unashamed
ask	v	reply, answer
asleep	adj	awake
attach	v	detach
attack	v	defend
attractive	adj	unattractive
autumn	n	spring
available	adj	unavailable
awake	adj	asleep
aware	adj	unaware
back	n	front
backward	adj	forward
bad	adj	good
ban	v	allow
banish	v	recall
barren	adj	fertile
base	n	top
beautiful	adj	ugly
before	adv	after
begin	v	end, cease, stop
behind	adv	in front, ahead
belief	n	disbelief
below	adv	above
bend	v	unbend, straighten
beneath	adv	above
best	adj	worst
better	adj	worse
big	adj	little
bitter	adj	sweet
black	adj	white
blind	adj	sighted
boastful	adj	modest
bold	adj	timid
bore	v	amuse

borrow	v	lend
bottom	n	top
bow	n	stern
brave	adj	cowardly
break	v	mend
bright	adj	dull, dim
brilliant	adj	dull
bring	v	take
brittle	adj	tough
broad	adj	narrow
build	v	destroy
busy	adj	idle
buy	v	sell
calm	adj	rough, angry
capable	adj	incapable
careful	adj	careless
careless	adj	careful, thoughtful
cause	n	effect
	v	prevent
cease	v	begin
certain	adj	uncertain
chaos	n	order
cheap	adj	expensive
cheerful	adj	sad
child	n	adult
clean	adj	dirty
clear	adj	unclear
clever	adj	stupid
climb	v	descend
close	v	open
clumsy	adj	agile
coarse	adj	fine
coil	v	uncoil
cold	adj	hot
collect	v	scatter
come	v	go
comfort	n	discomfort
comic	adj	tragic
common	adj	uncommon
complete	adj	incomplete
conceal	v	reveal
concern	n	unconcern
conduct	n	misconduct
connect	v	disconnect

content	n	discontent
continue	v	discontinue
contract	v	expand
convenient	adj	inconvenient
cool	adj	warm
correct	adj	incorrect
courage	n	cowardice
courteous	adj	discourteous
courtesy	n	discourtesy
cover	v	uncover
coward	n	hero
criminal	adj	lawful
cruel	adj	kind
cry	v	laugh
danger	n	safety
dark	adj	light, fair
dawn	n	dusk
day	n	night
dead	adj	alive
dear	adj	cheap
decent	adj	indecent
decrease	v	increase
deep	adj	shallow
defeat	n	victory
definite	adj	indefinite
demand	v, n	offer
deny	v	admit
depart	v	arrive
depth	n	height
descend	v	ascend
deserted	adj	occupied
desirable	adj	undesirable
despair	n, v	hope
die	v	live
difficult	adj	easy
dim	adj	bright
direct	adj	indirect
dirty	adj	clean
discipline	n	indiscipline
dismal	adj	bright
displease	v	please
distant	adj	near
distinct	adj	indistinct, unclear
distrust	n	trust

Opposites

doubtful	*adj*	certain
down	*adv*	up
draw	*v*	push
dreary	*adj*	bright
dress	*v*	undress
drop	*v*	pick up
drunk	*adj*	sober
dry	*adj*	wet
dwarf	*n*	giant
early	*adj*	late
ease	*n*	1 discomfort 2 difficulty
east	*n*	west
easy	*adj*	difficult
ebb	*n, v*	flow
edge	*n*	centre
educated	*adj*	uneducated
effect	*n*	cause
either	*adj, pron, adv*	neither
embark	*v*	disembark
empty	*v* *adj*	fill full
encourage	*v*	discourage
end	*v*	begin
enemy	*n*	friend
enlarge	*v*	reduce
enter	*v*	leave
entrance	*n*	exit
equal	*adj*	unequal
essential	*adj*	inessential
even	*adj*	uneven, odd
ever	*adv*	never
everywhere	*adv*	nowhere
evil	*n, adj*	good
exact	*adj*	inexact
excuse	*v*	accuse
exit	*n*	entrance
expand	*v*	contract
expensive	*adj*	inexpensive
expert	*adj*	inexpert
exterior	*n, adj*	interior
external	*adj*	internal
extraordinary	*adj*	ordinary

fact	*n*	fiction
fail	*v*	succeed
failure	*n*	success
faint	*adj*	clear
fair	*adj*	1 unfair 2 dark
faithful	*adj*	unfaithful
fake	*adj*	genuine
fall	*v*	rise
false	*adj*	true
familiar	*adj*	unfamiliar
far	*adj*	near
farther	*adv*	nearer
fast	*adj*	1 slow 2 loose
fasten	*v*	unfasten
fat	*adj*	thin
favourable	*adj*	unfavourable
feminine	*adj*	masculine
fertile	*adj*	infertile
fetch	*v*	take
few	*adj, pron*	many
fierce	*adj*	timid
fill	*v*	empty
final	*adj*	first, initial
find	*v*	lose
fine	*adj*	coarse
finish	*v*	start
first	*adj*	last, final
fit	*adj*	unfit
float	*v*	sink
flow	*v*	ebb
foe	*n*	friend
follow	*v*	lead
foolish	*adj*	wise
forbid	*v*	permit
forget	*v*	remember
former	*adj*	latter
fortunate	*adj*	unfortunate
foul	*adj*	fair
freeze	*v*	thaw
frequent	*adj*	infrequent
friend	*n*	foe

friendly	adj	unfriendly		**hindmost**	adj	foremost
from	prep	to, towards		**hit**	v	miss
front	n	back		**hold**	v	release
full	adj	empty		**hollow**	adj	solid
funny	adj	serious		**holy**	adj	unholy
				honest	adj	dishonest
gain	n	loss		**honour**	n	dishonour
gallant	adj	ungallant		**hope**	n	despair
gather	v	scatter		**hopeless**	adj	hopeful
gay	adj	miserable		**hostile**	adj	friendly
generous	adj	ungenerous, mean		**hot**	adj	cold
				human	adj	inhuman
genuine	adj	false		**humble**	adj	proud
giant	n	dwarf				
give	v	take, receive		**idiotic**	adj	sensible
glad	adj	sorry		**idle**	adj	busy
go	v	come		**ill**	adj	well
good	adj	bad		**illness**	n	health
gracious	adj	ungracious		**imaginary**	adj	real
grant	v	refuse		**immortal**	adj	mortal
grateful	adj	ungrateful		**impatient**	adj	patient
great	adj	small		**imperfect**	adj	perfect
ground	n	sky		**impolite**	adj	polite
grown-up	n	child		**important**	adj	unimportant
guilty	adj	innocent		**improper**	adj	proper
				improve	v	worsen
halt	v	go		**imprudent**	adj	prudent
happy	adj	unhappy		**impure**	adj	pure
hard	adj	1 soft 2 easy		**incorrect**	adj	correct
				increase	v	decrease
harmless	adj	harmful		**indecent**	adj	decent
hate	v, n	love		**indefinite**	adj	definite
head	n	tail		**indirect**	adj	direct
healthy	adj	unhealthy		**infirm**	adj	firm, healthy
heat	n	cold		**inhuman**	adj	human
heaven	n	hell		**innocent**	adj	guilty
heavy	adj	light		**inside**	n, adv, adj	outside
heed	v	ignore				
height	n	depth		**intelligent**	adj	unintelligent, stupid
hell	n	heaven				
help	v	hinder		**interior**	n, adj	exterior
helpful	adj	unhelpful		**inward**	adv	outward
here	adv	there				
heroic	adj	cowardly		**join**	v	part
high	adj	low		**junior**	adj, n	senior
hinder	v	help		**just**	adj	unjust

Jj Opposites Nn

justice	n	injustice
keen	adj	1 disinterested / 2 dull
kind	adj	unkind
land	v	1 board / 2 take off
large	adj	small
last	adj	first
late	adj	early
laugh	v	cry
lawful	adj	unlawful
lazy	adj	industrious, hard-working
lead	v	follow
leader	n	follower
lean	adj	fat
least	adj, n, adv	most
leave	v	arrive
left	adj, n, adv	right
leisure	n	work
lengthen	v	shorten
lenient	adj	strict
less	adj, n, adv	more
lie	n	truth
light	adj	1 dark / 2 heavy
like	v / adj	dislike / unlike
limp	adj	stiff
little	adj	big
live	adj / v	dead / die
long	adj	short
lose	v	1 find / 2 gain / 3 win
loser	n	winner
lot	n	few
loud	adj	soft
love	v	hate
low	adj	high
loyal	adj	disloyal

lucky	adj	unlucky
luxury	n	poverty
mad	adj	sane
male	n	female
man	n	woman
manage	v	mismanage
manhood	n	womanhood
many	adj	few
masculine	adj	feminine
master	n	slave
maximum	adj	minimum
mean	adj	generous
meaningless	adj	meaningful
messy	n	tidy
middle	n	outside
mild	adj	severe
minimum	adj	maximum
miserable	adj	happy
miss	v	hit
mix	v	separate
mock	adj	genuine
modern	adj	ancient
modest	adj	immodest
moist	adj	dry
more	adj, n, adv	less
most	adj, n, adv	least
mount	v	dismount
narrow	adj	wide
natural	adj	unnatural
near	adj	far
neat	adj	untidy
necessary	adj	unnecessary
neglect	v	care
neither	adj, pron, adv	either
never	adv	always
new	adj	old
nice	adj	nasty
night	n	day
no	adv	yes
noble	adj	ignoble

nobody	pron	somebody		**permanent**	adj	temporary
noise	n	silence		**permit**	v	forbid
none	pron	some		**place**	v	displace
nonsense	n	sense		**play**	n	work
normal	adj	abnormal		**pleasant**	adj	unpleasant
north	n	south		**please**	v	displease
notice	v	ignore, miss		**pleasing**	adj	displeasing
now	adv	then		**plentiful**	adj	scarce
nowhere	adv, pron	everywhere		**polite**	adj	impolite
nude	adj	clothed		**poor**	adj	1 rich, wealthy 2 good
numerous	adj	few		**popular**	adj	unpopular
				possible	adj	impossible
obedient	adj	disobedient		**poverty**	n	wealth
obey	v	disobey		**powerful**	adj	weak
object	v	approve, agree		**prepared**	adj	unprepared
observe	v	ignore		**present**	adj	absent
odd	adj	even		**pretty**	adj	ugly
off	adv, prep	on		**prevent**	v	permit
				priceless	adj	worthless
offend	v	please		**private**	adj	public
offer	v	demand		**probable**	adj	improbable
often	adv	seldom		**profit**	n	loss
old	adj	1 young 2 new		**prolong**	v	shorten
				promising	adj	unpromising
on	adv, prep	off		**prompt**	adj	late
				proper	adj	improper
onward	adv	backward		**proud**	adj	humble
open	adj	closed, shut		**prove**	v	disprove
optimistic	adj	pessimistic		**prudent**	adj	imprudent
order	n	disorder		**public**	adj	private
orderly	adj	disorderly		**pull**	v	push
ordinary	adj	extraordinary		**punish**	v	1 pardon 2 reward
out	adv	in				
outer	adj	inner		**purchase**	v	sell
outside	n	inside		**pure**	adj	impure
outward	adv	inward		**push**	v	pull
over	adj	under		**put**	v	take
pale	adj	bright		**question**	n, v	answer
part	v	join		**quick**	adj	slow
patient	adj	impatient		**quiet**	adj	noisy
peace	n	war				
peaceful	adj	noisy		**raise**	v	lower
peculiar	adj	normal		**rapid**	adj	slow
perfect	adj	imperfect		**rare**	adj	common

Opposites

rash	adj	cautious
raw	adj	cooked
ready	adj	unready
real	adj	unreal
reap	v	sow
rear	n	front
reasonable	adj	unreasonable
rebel	v	comply
receive	v	give
reckless	adj	cautious
recollect	v	forget
recover	v	lose
reduce	v	increase
refuse	v	accept
regular	adj	irregular
reject	v	accept
reliable	adj	unreliable
remarkable	adj	unremarkable, ordinary
remember	v	forget
remove	adj	replace
repair	v	damage
replace	v	remove
reply	n, v	question
resist	v	surrender
respect	n	disrespect
restful	adj	restless
restless	adj	restful
result	n	cause
retreat	v	advance
reveal	v	cover
rich	adj	poor
right	adj	wrong
	n, adj, v	left
rise	v	fall
rough	adj	smooth
rude	adj	polite
sad	adj	happy
safe	adj	unsafe
satisfactory	adj	unsatisfactory
savage	adj	tame
scarce	adj	plentiful
scatter	v	gather
secure	adj	unsafe, loose

seize	v	release
seldom	adv	often
selfish	adj	unselfish
sell	v	buy
send	v	receive
senior	n, adj	junior
sense	n	nonsense
senseless	adj	sensible
sensible	adj	senseless, stupid
settle	v	unsettle
severe	adj	gentle
shabby	adj	smart
shallow	adj	deep
sham	adj	real
shame	v	honour
sharp	adj	blunt
short	adj	1 long 2 tall
shortage	n	abundance
shout	v	whisper
show	v	conceal
shut	adj	open
shy	adj	confident
sincere	adj	insincere
sink	v	swim
skilful	adj	unskilful
slack	adj	tight
slim	adj	fat
slow	adj	fast
small	adj	large
smooth	adj	rough
sober	adj	drunk
soft	adj	hard
solid	adj	1 hollow 2 liquid
	n	liquid
soothe	v	vex
sorrow	n	joy
sour	adj	sweet
south	n	north
sow	v	reap
spend	v	save
spendthrift	n	miser
splendid	adj	dull
spring	n	autumn

stale	adj	fresh
start	v	finish
stay	v	leave
steady	adj	unsteady
stern	adj	friendly
	n	bow
stiff	adj	limp
still	adj	moving
stop	v	go
straight	adj	bent
strict	adj	lax
strong	adj	weak
stupid	adj	sensible
subtract	v	add
succeed	v	fail
success	n	failure
sudden	adj	gradual
suitable	adj	unsuitable
summer	n	winter
sure	adj	unsure
sweet	adj	sour
swift	adj	slow
swim	v	sink
tail	n	head
take	v	give
talkative	adj	quiet
tall	adj	short
tame	adj	wild
tasty	adj	tasteless
teach	v	learn
temporary	adj	permanent
tender	adj	tough
thankful	adj	unthankful
that	pron, adj	this
thaw	v	freeze
there	adv	here
these	pron, adj	those
thick	adj	thin
thin	adj	fat, thick
this	pron, adj	that
those	pron, adj	these
throw	v	catch

tidy	adj	untidy
tight	adj	loose
timid	adj	bold
tiny	adj	huge
to	prep	fro, from
toil	n, v	rest
top	n	bottom, base
tough	adj	tender
towards	prep	away from
tragic	adj	comic
treachery	n	loyalty
triumph	n	defeat
true	adj	untrue, false
trust	n, v	distrust, mistrust
trustworthy	adj	untrustworthy
truth	n	untruth, lie
try	v	fail
ugly	adj	beautiful, handsome
unable	adj	able
uncommon	adj	common
undecided	adj	decided
under	adv	over
underhand	adj	honest
undo	v	fasten
up	adv	down
upper	adj	lower
upward	adj, adv	downward
upwards	adv	downwards
urgent	adj	unimportant
use	v	misuse
	n	disuse
useful	adj	useless
useless	adj	useful
usual	adj	unusual
vacant	adj	engaged
valley	n	mountain
vanish	v	appear
vex	v	soothe
vice	n	virtue
victory	n	defeat
villain	n	hero

Vv   Opposites   Yy

violent	adj	calm	**wide**	adj	narrow
virtue	n	vice	**wild**	adj	tame
visible	adj	invisible	**win**	v	lose
vivid	adj	dull, pale	**wind**	v	unwind
			winner	n	loser
wane	v	wax	**winter**	n	summer
wanted	adj	unwanted	**wise**	adj	unwise
war	n	peace	**with**	prep	without
warm	adj	cold	**withdraw**	v	advance
wary	adj	unwary	**work**	n	play
waste	v	save, preserve	**worse**	adj	better
wasteful	adj	careful	**worst**	adj	best
wax	v	wane	**worthless**	adj	useful
weak	adj	strong	**wrap**	v	unwrap
wealth	n	poverty	**wrong**	adj	right
weary	adj	fresh			
well	adj	unwell	**yes**	adv	no
wet	adj	dry	**young**	adj	old
white	adj	black	**youth**	n	age
whole	n	part			
wicked	adj	good			

Making opposites

Some opposites may be made by using an affix, which is attached to either the front or the end of a word. For example, to make the opposite of *like* add the affix *dis* to produce *dislike*. The opposite of *careful* (*care* + *ful*) is *careless*. Here are some other examples.

Affix	Examples
ant-, anti-	arctic, antarctic clockwise, anticlockwise
dis-	like, dislike appear, disappear
im-	possible, impossible patient, impatient
in-	justice, injustice correct, incorrect
ir-	regular, irregular responsible, irresponsible
mis-	lead, mislead understand, misunderstand
non-	sense, nonsense member, non-member
un-	happy, unhappy do, undo
-ful, -less	careful, careless thoughtful, thoughtless

However, you must take great care when using affixes to make opposites, for they can sometimes be misleading. For example,

dislike is an opposite of *like*,

but *distant* is not an opposite of 'tant' – 'tant' is not a word;

injustice is an opposite of *justice*,

but *indeed* is not an opposite of *deed*, though *indeed* and *deed* are both words.

Designed by PFB Art & Type Limited, Shadwell, Leeds
Printed in England by Martin's The Printers Ltd, Berwick upon Tweed